D1287051

AMERICA'S
ECONOMIC STRENGTH

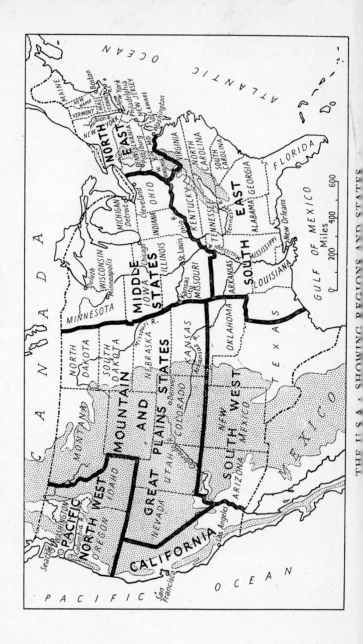

THE U.S.A. SHOWING REGIONS AND STATES

AMERICA'S ECONOMIC STRENGTH

By

C. J. HITCH

Fellow of The Queen's College, Oxford

OXFORD UNIVERSITY PRESS
LONDON · NEW YORK · TORONTO

OXFORD UNIVERSITY PRESS
AMEN HOUSE, E.C. 4
London Edinburgh Glasgow New York
Toronto Melbourne Capetown Bombay
Calcutta Madras
HUMPHREY MILFORD
PUBLISHER TO THE UNIVERSITY

First published January 1941
Reprinted . February 1941

62925

PRINTED IN GREAT BRITAIN

ACKNOWLEDGEMENT

I HAVE not tried to write an original book: the statistics have all been taken from other sources. I have, however, tried to write a readable book and I have therefore not distracted the reader's attention with footnotes and references. I am particularly indebted to Mr. Colin Clark, whose estimates of national income and its distribution by persons and occupations in *The Conditions of Economic Progress* form the basis of those I have given; and to *Fortune Magazine* for the figures on regional incomes and power consumption, as well as for permission to reproduce many of the Plates. I am also indebted to Professor Paul Douglas for much of the material in Graphs 10 and 11, to Dr. Harry Jerome for the figures on industrial power, to Mr. O. E. Baker for many of the agricultural statistics, and to Professor F. C. Mills for the price data incorporated in Graph 12. The other figures have been taken, in the main, from such official sources as the Publications of the United States Government, the Federal Reserve Board, and the League of Nations. I must ask a blanket pardon for adapting all statistics to my requirements, which I have done so freely that the original sources are thereby absolved of any responsibility for errors I may have committed.

Note

Readers who desire to study the basic factors of the American economy in more detail are recommended to consult: Charles and Mary Beard, *The Rise of*

American Civilization; Louis Hacker, *American Problems of Today*; E. D. Durand, *American Industry and Commerce*; A. E. Parkins and J. R. Whitaker (editors), *Our Natural Resources*; Nourse and others, *America's Capacity to Produce*; Colin Clark, *The Conditions of Economic Progress*; and *Recent Social Trends* and *Recent Economic Trends*, published by Committees set up by ex-President Hoover, many of the contributions to which, although slightly out of date, are better than anything which has been written since. Detailed works on the more topical subjects dealt with in Chapters IV, VI, and VII have not yet been published.

January 1941.

C. J. H.

CONTENTS

CHAP.   PAGE

I.	BACKGROUND	9
II.	NATURAL RESOURCES	32
III.	MANUFACTURING INDUSTRY	45
IV.	WAR INDUSTRIES	60
V.	DEPRESSION AND NEW DEAL	74
VI.	WAR	95
VII.	AMERICA AND THE BRITISH EMPIRE	102
	INDEX	111

ILLUSTRATIONS

PLATE   PAGE

I.	HIGH INCOMES	23
II.	LOW INCOMES	25
III.	CONTRASTS IN AGRICULTURE	33
IV.	NATURAL PRODUCTS	41
V.	EXTREMES OF MODERN MANUFACTURING	49
VI.	IRON ORE COMES BY THE GREAT LAKES	58
VII.	AID FOR BRITAIN	65
VIII.	NEW DEAL PUBLIC WORKS	89

MAP

THE U.S.A.: SHOWING REGIONS AND STATES *Frontispiece*

CHAPTER I

BACKGROUND

ECONOMIC strength, whether of an individual or a nation, is unfortunately not a quantity which can be measured in tons or money or any other single dimension. The concept is itself ambiguous, for the strength available may depend to a very great extent upon the purpose for which it is to be used. Strength to raise standards of living does not necessarily mean strength of the sort which is effective in diplomacy; still less, as the history of the past years has tragically demonstrated, does it imply power to wage war.

The purpose of this book is to examine the economic organization of the United States of America, and to assess and explain its strength in the varied senses of that term. Fortunately there is, underlying these various senses, a common factor which simplifies our task: the *potential* economic strength of a nation for any purpose depends upon its ability to produce goods and services, and this in turn depends upon its natural resources, its accumulated wealth, and the number and character of its population. The ability to use this potential strength for any particular purpose will depend upon a variety of special factors—upon the precise types of goods and services which its industry is equipped to produce, upon the length of time available to transfer resources from one kind of production to another, and upon the will, intelligence, and adaptability of the Government, business, and labour. Our first task is to examine America's potential economic strength, her power to produce goods and services in general. In later chapters we shall consider her ability to produce those specific goods and services which are most useful for war purposes.

Now, *ability* to produce goods and services in general is a difficult thing to measure. Nations may be unaware of their own strength in time of need. If we are to avoid discussing the subject in vague generalities we must begin with something concrete: with the goods and services *actually produced*. We can then make some sort of estimate of the extent to which actual production falls short of capacity.

The sum total of goods and services produced in a country is called by economists the "national income". It is a technical term, and there are difficulties in its exact definition which need not concern us. But the underlying concept is a simple one, and we shall make extensive use of it. All goods and services produced are valued in terms of money, and the total values added together. In order to make it possible to compare the national incomes of different countries, or of the same country at different times, goods are valued at the same prices irrespective of where or when they are produced. In this book we shall use the prices ruling in pre-war Britain [1] for this purpose, since readers probably have a fairly clear recollection of what the pre-war pound would buy.

Total national income is divided up among the people who produce it. "Income per occupied person" is simply national income divided by the number of occupied persons. By "occupied persons" in this book we mean the total labour force—wage-earners, salaried workers, farmers, and business men, whether they are actually working or unemployed at any par-

[1] More specifically, those ruling in 1937. It is estimated that the 1937 pound is the equivalent of 5·5 of the "international units" used by Mr. Colin Clark in *The Conditions of Economic Progress*.

ticular time. National income can be interpreted as a sort of rough measure of economic power; income per occupied person as a measure of " opulence ".

In comparing the incomes of different countries it is best to take the average of a number of years, because in any single year some countries are likely to be exceptionally prosperous or exceptionally depressed. Graph 1 shows the average national incomes of a number of important countries in the decade 1925–34,

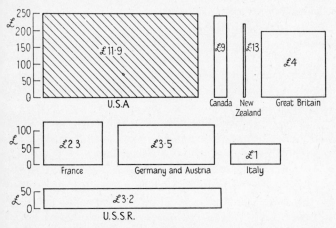

1. National Incomes (1925–34 average) shown by the size of rectangle. Average income per occupied person is measured vertically, the occupied population horizontally.

which affords a good basis for comparison, since it covered, in every country, a period of prosperity and one of depression. National income is represented by the size of the rectangle, income per occupied person by its height, and the occupied population by its breadth. The United States is clearly, as some American politicians are fond of boasting, the " richest and most powerful " economic unit in the world. Its national income in this period averaged just short of twelve thousand million pounds, as compared with four thousand million for the United Kingdom, 3·5 for Germany, 3·2 for Russia, and 2·3 for France. If we exclude India and China, with their enormous populations but undeveloped economies, for which no reasonably comparable figures exist, no other nation in the world has an income approaching these. The power of the United States to produce economic goods and services was almost as great as that of the next four most important world Powers combined, and slightly greater than that of the whole of continental Europe.

The comparisons of income per occupied person, represented on Graph 1 by the height of the rectangles, show that Americans are also the richest people in the world, but that their superiority is nothing like as marked as some of Hollywood's productions might suggest. Average income per occupied person was £250 in the United States, as compared with £195 in Great Britain. The closest approach to the American standard was found in the British Dominions.

Since 1934 there has been a general increase in national incomes as countries have recovered from the great depression, and it has been accompanied by some shifts in the relative incomes of different countries. Income per occupied person in Great Britain, Germany, Australia, and New Zealand has increased more rapidly than in the United States and Canada, largely because of the continued existence of large-scale unemployment in North America. The 1937 figures for Great Britain and the United States were £232 and £256 respectively, and it is possible that the New Zealand figure was slightly higher. But, for reasons already mentioned, the average for the 1925–34 decade provides a better basis for comparison than any later year. Actual output in the United States in the period since 1934 has fallen below potential output by a larger percentage than in any other country. We tend to think that the unemployment figure in Great Britain in recent years has been high, but in 1937 the United States, with three times the British population, had six times as many unemployed, and millions on short time. We can get some idea of *ability* to produce, as opposed to actual production, by measuring income per person working a full normal week: in the United States in 1937 the fully employed worker produced on the average goods and services worth £340; in Great Britain, £260. This may somewhat exaggerate the difference, because unemployed labour is less efficient than employed, but the error is not large.

National income, even if we include the potential production of the unemployed and under-employed, is only a rough index of general economic strength, and one very important reservation must be borne in mind in comparing the areas in Graph 1. A very large proportion of national income consists of goods and services which are necessary for bare subsistence, and which are not therefore a source of strength for any other purpose. It has been estimated that the national income of China is about the same as that of Britain, but since almost all of it is required to feed, clothe, and house 450,000,000 Chinese, the surplus available for waging war or doing anything else is a fraction of Britain's. If, instead of comparing national incomes, we could compare potential national incomes in excess of what is required for subsistence, the superiority of the United States would appear much greater.

This is shown most strikingly by figures for the production of the commodities which people buy when they have satisfied the more urgent needs of existence: luxuries, or what were once considered luxuries; and capital goods,[1] in which savings are invested. The

---

[1] *i.e.*, factories and other buildings, machines, railways, power plants, etc. as opposed to money capital.

luxuries are less important for war purposes; the fact
that Americans own 95% of the world's bathtubs [1]
would not deter a would-be aggressor. But the
economic resources producing many luxuries could
easily be released and transferred to other work.
America produces over two-thirds of the world's motor-
cars, which means that, starting from scratch, she
could produce airplanes, tanks, and army transport
vehicles on a larger scale in shorter time than any
other country. The capital-goods industries are more
directly relevant to a war economy, since they provide
the essential materials, tools, and power. No single
figure can summarize the strength of the American
economy in this field, but an indication is given by the
fact that, with 7% of the world's population, it produces
a third of the world's coal, a third of its iron and steel,
60% of its oil, and generates a third of its electric
power.

There is a widespread belief that the high American
standard of life is a recent development. It is true that
American industrial development has been recent and
extremely rapid: in the nineteenth century American
industry was an unimportant satellite of European
industry; by the 1920's it had surpassed European
industry both in scale and in technique. It is also
true that as a result of the World War America ceased
to be a debtor and became a creditor nation. But these
two developments, which seem so striking and important,
have had surprisingly little effect in raising the level of
American income. The margin of superiority of the
American standard of life over the European was more
marked in 1850 than it is today.

The development of income per occupied person
in the United States is traced in Graph 2, curve (A).
In 1850 its value, in pre-war pounds, was £143, and
it rose steadily, apart from a brief interruption due

[1] See Plate VII, p. 65.

to the Civil War, while the West was being settled. By 1900 it had reached the high figure of £250, which is approximately the level at which it stands today. The reason for the high average income of the latter half of the nineteenth century was a simple one: the prosperity of the dominant industry, agriculture. America was the first great overseas producer of agricultural products to be developed, and for a time

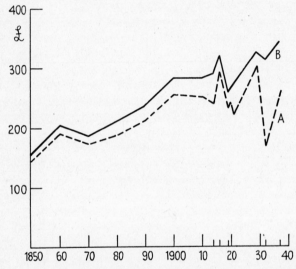

2. Income per occupied person in U.S.A. 1850–1937. (A) shows income per employable person, (B) income per worker in a full working week. Loss of income through unemployment and short time, represented by distance between curves, has been a major problem since 1929.

she was able to sell them on European markets at highly remunerative prices. In the twentieth century the rapid development of industry has done little more than offset the declining prosperity of agriculture. There was some increase in average income during the World War due to the absorption of the unemployed, but it was more than lost in the post-war slump. The transition from international debtor to international creditor had little or no effect, because America refused to accept the imports by which her credits could be repaid. From 1922 to 1929 there was recovery and sustained prosperity for most sections of the community, and in 1929 American income per occupied person reached a new high, for America and the world, of just under £300. But in the autumn of the same year the Great Depression started, and average income· fell precipitately to £170 in 1932. Recovery has been slow, and even in 1937, now recognized as the top of a minor boom, income per head was still well below the 1929 level.

This brief account of the development of the American economy in terms of income per head is in several respects misleading. Productivity, as opposed to actual income, or production, was increasing rapidly and fairly steadily during the whole period from 1850 to 1937. Productivity may be measured in two ways: per week and per hour. Productivity per worker in a normal working week is traced on Graph 2, curve (B). It increased, as a rule, even during depressions, and in 1937 exceeded £340, higher than it had ever been in the past. The difference between this figure and income per occupied person is accounted for by unemployment and short-time working, which in America more than anywhere else in the world has become the most pressing problem of economic organization. Productivity per hour is not shown on the graph; it has increased even more spectacularly than productivity per week. While the latter doubled between 1850 and 1937, the former increased threefold. The difference in this case is not a problem of organization; it simply reflects the desire of American labour, like English labour, to take a part of its gain from increased productivity in the form of increased leisure rather than in a larger flow of goods and services.

In another respect this historical sketch understates the progress made by the American economy in recent decades. Since 1900 there has been a great increase in the variety of goods and services from which consumers can choose. An " occupied person " in 1900 might have had an income which would buy as great a quantity of certain 1937 goods as an occupied person in 1937 could buy with his income. But there were many goods available to the 1937 consumer which no practicable amount of money could have purchased in 1900—motor-cars, wireless sets, telephones, labour-saving household equipment, and indeed most of the commodities which we tend to think of as characteristic of modern American consumption. Wealth depends upon variety as well as upon quantity, and income figures of the sort we have quoted do not and cannot fully reflect this important factor.

The increase in output, income, and productivity which has taken place during the last hundred years has been accompanied by great changes in the relative importance of different industries and occupations. Graph 3 shows the changes in the proportion of the total occupied population engaged in the primary industries, manufacturing, and the provision of services since 1870. In this period America has rapidly passed through all the stages of economic development. At the end of the Civil War it was still predominantly rural and agricultural. The industrial revolution had just begun. Over half the population was engaged in the primary extractive industries—agriculture, forestry, and fishing; and of these agriculture was by far the most important. The American standard of living was the highest of any nation, not because America was more progressive, but because the land was fertile and abundant, and the European market had not yet been glutted by surpluses from

B   (U. S. A. 2)

other overseas regions. America is still the leading
agricultural producer in the world, but the relative
importance of agriculture in the American economy
has steadily declined. From 70% a century ago,
and 54% in 1870, the proportion of the occupied
population engaged in agriculture fell to 23% in 1930.
During the depression of the '30's there was a slight
increase as a result of unemployed labour turning to

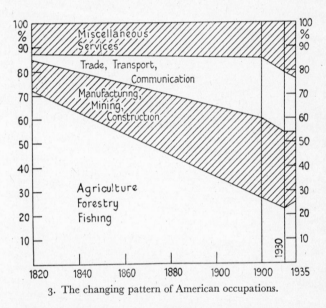

3. The changing pattern of American occupations.

subsistence farming, but there is no doubt that a
return of prosperity would further reduce the proportion.

The development of American industry in the
narrower sense—manufacturing, mining, and building—was continuous, as measured by the occupation
census, until 1920. The proportion of the occupied
population engaged in industry is shown on Graph 3.
It increased from 23% in 1870 to a peak of 33% in

1920, and has since declined to just over a quarter. This development is entirely normal. The great increases in productivity which we have already traced were largely concentrated in manufacturing industry; and it has become possible for a smaller proportion of the population to produce more and more things—steel, motor-cars, and soap—*per capita*. There is a limit to the number of things people want; as their incomes increase they spend them in an increasing proportion on services.

The provision of these services has accounted for the other great shift in the distribution of the working population. In 1870 less than a quarter of the occupied population was engaged in the service industries —trade, transport, communications, and personal and professional services. Today the proportion, represented by the top two areas in Graph 3, has doubled, and there is every indication that it will continue to increase. Half the service employees are engaged in transport, communications, and wholesale and retail trade; the other half in a very miscellaneous and ill-defined collection of occupations—government and administrative services, the hotel, catering, and personal service trades, the various professions and near-professions, and domestic service. All of these except the last, which is much less important than in England and declining, are rapidly expanding. Their relative prosperity in recent years has prevented the unemployment problem from becoming catastrophic.

This, then, is the pattern of American occupations: a bare and declining quarter engaged in agriculture and other primary industries; another declining quarter in mining, manufacturing, and building; a third quarter, which may or may not have reached its peak, in trade, transport, and communication; and a fourth quarter, destined to become larger, in supplying miscellaneous services. This occupational pattern differs from the British in only one striking particular; here only 6% are engaged in agriculture, and 44% in manufacturing, building, and mining. If half those employed in manufacturing industry were transferred to agriculture the proportions in each of the broad divisions would be the same in Great Britain as in the United States.

Figures of average income of the sort we have been discussing conceal quite as much of the truth as they reveal. Very few people receive the average income: most receive less, a few receive a great deal more. There are great differences in income—between individuals, occupations, and regions—and these are as marked in America as in any other country. The individual differences are common knowledge: America of the films is a land of millionaires and dispossessed, with the millionaires losing ground to the dispossessed since the prosperous '20's, and the picture is not unfair. The distribution of personal incomes in the United States is almost as unequal as in Great Britain.

The wide differences by occupations and regions are not as generally appreciated. One might expect from the rapidly declining proportion of the population engaged in it that agriculture is the least profitable of American occupations, and this is the case, as Graph 4 shows. American agriculture is neither as productive nor as profitable for those engaged in it as the agriculture of Australia and New Zealand, and little more productive than that of some European countries. The great depressed industries of England since the World War have been coal, textiles, and shipbuilding. These were depressed in America as well, for similar reasons, but they were not as depressed as agriculture, nor did their depression affect as many people. The great rise in agricultural prices during the war (see Graph 12, p. 83) led to an expansion of production throughout the world, including Europe, which had been America's best market; and prices have not yet recovered from their collapse in the post-war slump. Even during the '20's, the greatest era of American prosperity, mortgages were being foreclosed and thousands of banks were failing in the agricultural regions. Within agriculture there are

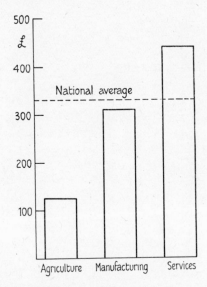

4. Average income by occupations, 1935. The height of the bars represents the earnings of fully employed persons.

important differences: citrus fruits and dairy products are profitable, and in the more fertile regions of the Middle West farmers do not live in penury. But in many regions—particularly in the South and in the increasingly arid regions of the Western plains—the plight of the producers of the great staple agricultural products is, relatively to their more fortunate fellow countrymen, a desperate one.

When we turn to the other occupations—manufacturing industry and the services—we find a very different picture. Productivity in American manufacturing industry is the highest in the world—more than twice as high as in Great Britain, and approached only in the Dominions. The income of the quarter of the population engaged in manufacturing, mining, and building is more twice as great as the income of the quarter engaged in agriculture, fishing, and

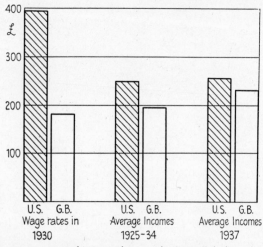

5. Average wages and average incomes in Great Britain and U.S.A.

(1) Average wage-rates of comparatively skilled workers, 1930.
(2) Average income per occupied person, 1925–34.
(3) Average income per occupied person, 1937.

forestry. A striking illustration of these occupational differences is afforded by Graph 5, which compares American wage-rates and average incomes with the British. In Britain, as in most industrial countries, income per occupied person is about equal to the average wages of fully employed skilled and semi-skilled workers. But in America, while average income is only slightly greater than in Britain, wage-rates are more than twice as high. The average British work-

I. HIGH INCOMES

**SKILLED
LABOUR**
Ewing Galloway)

**WINTER
VEGETABLES
IN
CALIFORNIA**
(Paul Popper)

DISTRIBUTION
(Ewing Galloway)

man (skilled and semi-skilled) was earning just over £3 10s. per week in 1930, the average American workman over £7; and the position of American unskilled labour was relatively slightly more favourable. Average American income is low, relatively to the British, because, unlike Britain, America has a great impoverished rural population. In recent years the gap between wage-rates and incomes in America has widened because of the unprecedented volume of unemployment.

The profitability of providing services in America is even greater than that of manufacturing. This reflects the greatly increased demand for their provision in the last two decades, and accounts for the steady transfer to the service trades and professions of persons from other occupations. In the case of manufacturing it was possible to attribute a large part of the profitability of American industry to its high productivity. Whether Americans are equally efficient in providing services is much more difficult to say, because of the impossibility, in most cases, of defining and measuring a "unit" of service. In one field, however, that of retail distribution, comparisons are feasible, for we can measure the number of goods delivered and the number of man-hours engaged in delivering them. Here it is clear that great progress in efficiency has been made during the last thirty years, due chiefly to the development of "chain stores" (multiple shops); and that American efficiency is far greater than British.

The wide variations in income by occupations are reflected in variations by regions which are only slightly less marked. We are familiar with regional variations in income in Great Britain: there are depressed areas and prosperous ones. But by comparison with the United States, the British economy could be described as uniform. It is customary for persons writing of the United States to emphasize that it is not a country but

II. LOW INCOMES

1. UNEMPLOYED SEEKING JOBS IN NEW YORK HARBOUR (*Mondiale*)

2. POOR FARMING FAMILY IN SOUTH-EAST (*Eliot Elisofon, from " Fortune "*)

a continent. Economically it is not a unit, but a collection of diversified regional economies.[1] It is possible to make, for each of these, a rough estimate of income per occupied person, and Graph 6 plots these estimates together with the American and British averages for purposes of comparison. The regional differences are due in part to varying natural resources and populations (Negroes are numerous in the South-east, Mexicans in the South-west); but in the main they simply reflect the varying proportions of persons en-

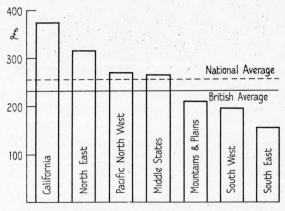

6. Regional variations in income, 1937.

gaged in the more profitable and less profitable occupations. Differences in standards of living are not quite as pronounced as differences in income, for the cost of living is lowest in the South-east, and highest in California and the Pacific North-west.

The North-east—New England and the industrial states of New York, Pennsylvania, and New Jersey— stands in much the same relation to the other regions as England does to the Empire. It imports much of its food from them, and most of its raw materials except

[1] See Map, frontispiece.

coal, and exports steel, machinery, and manufactured goods. Agriculture is unimportant, and income per head correspondingly high.

In most striking contrast stands the South-east—the "Old South"—which, despite the development of textile and other industries in recent years, is still pre-dominantly agricultural. It exports its staples—cotton and tobacco—as well as lumber, coal, and crude oil, and imports finished products. Its *per capita* income is less than half that of the North-east. That the large Negro element in the population is not wholly responsible is proved by the fact that hundreds of thousands of white tenant farmers engaged in the same occupation as most of the Negroes are able to earn no higher incomes.

The Middle States, extending from Ohio to the Western Plains, possess by far the best balanced of the American regional economies, and the only one which is reasonably self-sufficient. Its agricultural land is fertile, and much of it is devoted to the more profitable types of agricultural production, such as dairying. Its pattern of occupations corresponds closely to the American average, and its *per capita* income is slightly higher.

Lying beyond the Middle States is the Great Plains region of Kansas, Nebraska, and the Dakotas, and west of this is the Rocky Mountain region. Comprising more than a quarter of the total area of the United States, these areas support 5% of the population on something like 4% of the national income. The principal products are all primary—minerals, livestock, and grain, much of the latter grown on arid land which during the drought of the 1930's has become unsuited for cultivation.

The South-west—West Texas, Oklahoma, New Mexico, and Arizona—is a similar region. Petroleum is its great export industry, with livestock and mining subsidiary. Cotton, citrus fruits, and winter vegetables are grown in the relatively small areas where rainfall is adequate or irrigation possible.

California is a region in itself, with a *per capita* income higher than any other, and almost half again as high as the American average. The explanation is only in part occupational, in the broad sense in which we have been using the term. It is largely due to the fact that within each of the occupational groups California concentrates her efforts on the newest, most exotic, and profitable sorts of production. Her important agricultural crops are citrus fruits, winter vegetables, and wine grapes. Her important industries are the cinema and aircraft. Her important minerals are petroleum and gold. Her services are " exported " to tourists, and consumed internally by hundreds of thousands of wealthy and middle-class people who have retired to California from all parts of the country, taking with them their accumulated capital and its annual income.

The Pacific North-west, consisting of Washington, Idaho, and Oregon, is an example of a region engaged chiefly in primary production of a fairly profitable type for which its natural resources are ideally suited. Its principal exports to other regions are lumber, its by-products, wheat, and apples; and it is able, despite the dangerous lack of balance in its economy, to secure an income somewhat in advance of the national average.

It is clear from this brief review of occupations and regions that there is nothing uniform about America's economic superiority. The quarter of the population engaged in primary production are not strikingly more successful in their economic endeavours than people in similar occupations in Europe, and a good deal less successful than those in the Dominions, where extensive agricultural production is possible in even more favourable circumstances. There are exceptions to this statement: some agricultural crops in some regions yield high returns. But in general the factors which make the American economy the richest and strongest in the world must be sought elsewhere.

These factors operate most conspicuously in the field of manufacturing industry, where the productivity of labour is much greater than in any other country. They are also to be found in mining, and probably, although the facts are not clear, in the provision of certain important services.

The reasons for the greater productivity of American labour in these industries are numerous and their inter-relations are complex. They are environmental, social, and political in character, for the racial composition of America differs so little from that of Britain and Western Europe that it is futile to search for explanations in that direction.

Undoubtedly the abundant natural resources of the continent, developed long before similar resources in the Dominions and South America, were responsible for the early achievement of a high standard of life in America. We shall examine these resources, or what is left of them, in the next chapter. The indirect effects of these resources on the quality of labour and the accumulation of capital are now even more important than the resources themselves.

A great deal of nonsense has been talked about the American doctrine of high wages which is associated with the name of Henry Ford, but it is probably true that much of the energy, the adaptability, and the resourcefulness of American labour is due to the fact that it has in the past been paid more than labour in other countries. It was not paid more for this reason: it was paid more because it was more productive and because the accessibility of the " frontier " forced employers to make wage-rates attractive; but the effect of paying it more is that it is now still more productive.

This early high standard of life also made possible the accumulation of capital, in the form of railways, machines, and factories. People with high incomes tend to save and invest a larger proportion of them, and there were fewer exceptions to this rule in the Victorian age, which was America's as well as England's, than there are today. And the accumulation of capital, once started, is cumulative, for by increasing productivity it increases surpluses for further investment. A major part of the explanation of the greater productivity of American labour today is that each labourer is working with more capital—more machines, more mechanical power—than the average labourer of any other country.

There are also non-economic factors which are no less important because it is impossible to measure them. American business men, as well as American labourers, are readier to adopt new methods, more impatient with conventions and regulations, than their European counterparts, and much more so than their British counterparts. The development of the western frontier and the psychological attitudes which it created are probably largely responsible; and, going farther back, the fact that America was settled by immigrants from Europe who hated tradition in most of its forms. Some new indigenous traditions have since grown up, but most are still fluid, and not restrictive of business enterprise. Nowhere in the world has the task of the trade union organizer, or the organizer of industrial cartels, been beset with so many difficulties, and, until very recently, achieved so little success. Nowhere in the world is so much spent on industrial research for new products and new processes.

No account of the factors which contribute to America's economic strength would be complete, however, without the greatest stress being placed on the fact of political and economic union. America is not strong because each or some of the regions which we discussed contain elements of strength; it is strong because each is able to contribute to the others and the whole. Without unity the North-east would be an England, the South-east a Poland, the Middle West a Germany, and the Far West a Siberia. That this has not happened is due to two events which occurred at the end of the eighteenth century: one primary, the adoption of the Federal Constitution; the second subsidiary, the inclusion in that constitution of an economic clause entrusting the Federal Government with the regulation of interstate commerce, and forbidding the States to levy tariffs on it. The Federal Government's regulation has, for the most part, taken the form of active encouragement: it subsidized the early railways by grants of land, and has spent large sums in the improvement of through highways and the development of air transport. Important producing interests in some States have persuaded their legislatures to attempt to circumvent the ban on interstate tariffs by various subterfuges: the depression of the 1930's marked the appearance of inspection stations at state boundaries ostensibly to prevent the import of infected produce, and of a spate of excises on goods competing with the staples of the states levying them. But the total effect of these measures has been small. The Federal Constitution succeeded in creating the greatest area of free trade in the world, in which an extensive, if not perfect, division of labour enabled each region and each state to specialize in the production of the goods which it was best suited to make, and which made possible the utilization of the nation's capital for the efficient manufacture of commodities on a mass production scale.

CHAPTER II

NATURAL RESOURCES

NATURAL resources were once the chief basis of America's economic strength. This is no longer true, partly because of the rapid advance of industry, partly because the resources have been exploited with carelessness and waste. This chapter will examine the present state of America's resources— her land, forests, minerals, and natural power—and the agricultural and extractive industries directly engaged in developing them.

In the nineteenth century the abundance of fertile land in the East, the Middle West, and the South gave the American farmer and plantation-owner a great advantage over their Old-World rivals, and, as we have seen, the production and export of vast quantities of basic agricultural products—grains and cotton—largely accounted for the remarkably high American standard of life. America still produces a larger agricultural output than any other country, but in every other respect the situation has altered. The opening up of new territory in Canada, South America, and the Pacific, much of it better suited than most American land for the staple crops, and the growth of " autarchy " in Europe in recent years, have largely destroyed the foreign market for American produce. At the same time the remarkable progress of manufacturing industry, the shift in demand from things to services, and improvements in agricultural technique which have enabled fewer farmers to supply the needs of an increasing population, have made

III. CONTRASTS IN AGRICULTURE

1. A FARM IN THE "DUST BOWL" (*Ewing Galloway*)

2 & 3. OLD AND NEW FARMING METHODS

(*F. S. Lincoln.   Torkel Korling, from " Fortune "*)

agriculture the least remunerative of all the major branches of American industry. The quarter of the population engaged in agriculture receive today only 15% of the national income. Since 1930 about 27% of all farms have been subject to foreclosure and forced sale.

Concepts based on the position in the nineteenth century still persist, and the decline in the relative standing of American agriculture is not generally realized. American farming, on the average, is not

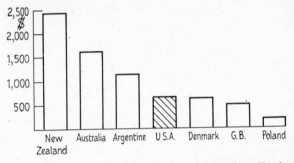

7. The agricultural productivity of selected countries. Total production in each country, valued at average American prices 1925–34, has been divided by the number of men engaged in agriculture. Dutch productivity is about the same as Danish, French and German about the same as British. The Polish figure is representative of peasant productivity.

efficiently conducted. Graph 7 measures the relative output per man engaged in agriculture in a number of countries. American productivity is far below that in newer regions, and little higher than that of Western European countries. This may be surprising to those whose acquaintance with American agriculture is limited to pictures of vast grain-fields and spectacular modern farm machinery. Both exist: but the typical American farm is small, and uses no power except the muscles of men and animals.

There are several reasons for the poor showing of

American agriculture. One is that America no longer possesses much good agricultural land in proportion to her population. She has perhaps 4% or 5% of the world total, which is less than her share and much less proportionately than that possessed by the Dominions and the Argentine. For this the American farmer can blame his ancestors, who depleted the virgin land by intensive cultivation of single crops, did nothing to restore its fertility, and permitted the wind and the rain to erode much of the topsoil which remained.

A second reason for the inferior productivity of American agriculture is the continued use of anti-quated methods of farming. Farmers are everywhere conservative, and although the American farmer likes to think of himself as a modern business man, and is popularly supposed to be more adaptable than the farmers of Europe, the fact that farming methods were developed at an early stage in American history still has a depressing effect on average productivity. Millions are spent each year by the Department of Agriculture and by the agricultural institutes of American universities in attempts to improve methods and educate farmers in their use, but lack of imagination and lack of capital have proved powerful enemies. Today only 14% of American farms have tractors, 16% electricity, and 19% motor lorries. Holland and Denmark are special cases of old agricultural countries thoroughly and intelligently organized for the production of certain products for which they have special advantages; nevertheless their agricultural productivity is even lower than that of the United States.

In part the explanation of Graph 7 lies in the misleading computation of an average for the whole of the United States. Regional and individual differences are striking. It is again the Old South which is largely responsible for the lowness of the average. With half the total farming population, it produces only 30% of the farm income. Its farms are the smallest in the country (71 acres is the average size); it has suffered most from erosion (45% of all eroded land is in the South-east); its methods are the most primitive (2·4% of Southern farms have tractors, compared with 14% of all farms); its ratio of tenancy (about 50%) is higher than that of any other region, and increasing. Over a million tenant farmers, and five times as many persons, most of them white, using no capital and too little land, eke out an existence from cotton or tobacco which would be considered inadequate by an unemployed labourer in Western Europe.[1] Many are " sharecroppers ", paying their rent with a percentage " share " of the crop. It is no wonder that the South has come to be known in recent years as America's " No. 1 " economic problem.

Another submarginal agricultural region, but of a different sort, is the semi-arid western part of the Great Plains, where the expansion of acreage resulting from the World War took place. This region should never have been ploughed. Its moisture has always been inadequate, and the destruction of grass further reduced rainfall and lowered the level of the sub-surface water. The drought of the last ten years has made what might have been reasonably good pasture an eroded, depleted " Dust Bowl " (see Plate III). From it the best surface soil has blown to the Middle West in great dust-storms, which have been one of the most spectacular sights on the continent in recent years—the only one of which Americans are not proud. The ruined farms are slowly being aban-doned, and many of the farmers have, like the " Okies " of Steinbeck's *Grapes of Wrath*, joined the migrant

[1] See Plate II, p. 25.

agricultural labourers in California. The 1940 census shows that the States in the tier from Oklahoma to North Dakota were the only ones which declined in population during the preceding decade.

By contrast, the grain and dairy farms of the Middle States are reasonably prosperous. Thirty-three per cent. of the farm population lives here, and produces 40% of the farm income. But by far the most prosperous farmers live in California, where the *per capita* farm income is four times the national average, and higher than anywhere else in the world. California farms are large; many are " capitalistic " both in their methods and their organization. The principal products are citrus fruits and winter vegetables,[1] which are " money " crops, suitable for large-scale production with seasonal hired labour. Farm income is badly distributed, for the pressure of migrant labour from other regions has enabled owners to pay low wages.

There has been some increase in the productivity of American agriculture, although it has been much less spectacular than in the case of manufacturing industry. Between 1900 and 1930 the number of persons engaged in agriculture increased by a tenth, while agricultural production increased 50%. In recent years the gains in productivity have been of a rather odd sort. Yields per acre of the major crops, which were always low, have declined slightly, due to erosion and depletion of the soil. But there have been shifts from less profitable to more profitable crops—from wheat to maize, from grains to fruits and vegetables, and from beef-cattle to dairy-cattle and pigs. At the same time *net* output of grains has increased as tractors have replaced horses and mules; and improved methods and strains have increased the amount of meat and milk produced from a pound of animal feed.

[1] See Plate I, p. 23.

The consumption per head of foodstuffs has been remarkably constant since 1900 at a level about equal to that of Sir John Orr's " optimum " diet; *i.e.*, one which furnishes all the essential calories, vitamins, and minerals. The very unequal distribution of income, however, means that excessive consumption by certain classes is balanced by malnutrition among the unemployed and the impoverished agricultural producers. There have been important shifts in consumption since 1900 within the total, corresponding to the shifts in production already mentioned. The characteristic and the most important American food is milk: the milk bar of the " corner drug store " is the American substitute for " pubs " and fish-and-chip shops. Consumption per head was 12·5 pints a week in 1900, and has since increased to 13 (the British average is now 4·1). The consumption of meat, high by European standards in 1900, has since remained roughly constant at 2·7 pounds; but the consumption of cereals has fallen from 7·3 pounds to 5. Consumption of sugar has increased by 50%. The total consumption of fruit has remained roughly constant, but citrus fruits and grapes have replaced apples; and the same sort of shift has occurred in the consumption of vegetables, where potatoes have been replaced by peas, beans, tomatoes, lettuce, artichokes, avocados, and asparagus.

America still produces for export a surplus of a few agricultural products. Cotton and wheat are the most important, and maize, tobacco, pork, and fruits are next. Imports, on a value basis, are now somewhat greater; the most important, in order, being coffee, sugar, silk, rubber, bananas, cocoa, wool, linseed, hides, and tea. Perhaps the most important conclusion, from our point of view, is that America is still almost self-sufficient in foodstuffs, and largely self-sufficient in the agricultural raw materials; and that the deficiencies, with the exception of rubber and possibly silk, can be made good from easily accessible regions in Latin America, or are non-essentials.

Possible exports are not unimportant. Production of many staples has been limited or reduced as a deliberate policy of the Federal Government since the beginning of the depression (see Chapter V), and if markets or needs arose could be quickly expanded. Graph 8 shows current production as a percentage of world production. The U.S. still produces the bulk of the world's cotton, could produce much more, and has a year's output in stocks. It is still the leading producer of dairy products and maize, and ranks second or third in many other staples, including wheat and meat. Production of these, too, could be increased, and the carry-overs of the grains are very large.

Forestry, like agriculture, is an industry the relative importance of which has been declining. Production of lumber and other forestry products in the past has been enormous, due largely to the demand for wood as a building material. Annual cuttings have exceeded annual growth, and there has also been careless waste of forest resources in cutting and clearing. It is estimated that half the continental area of the U.S. was once in trees; today the proportion is under a quarter, and only half of this represents forests suitable for timber. The long-run position is not as unfavourable as these figures might suggest, however, because the use of wood in construction has been declining since the early years of this century, and will probably continue to decline. Wood is a suitable building material for a new community, which must erect large numbers of houses quickly and cheaply, but it is in many respects inferior to stone, metals, brick, and cement. As the demand for lumber for building has declined the demand for wood-pulp for making paper has increased, but since the kinds of trees most suitable for pulping are not grown extensively in the States, it is necessary to import more than half the amount required, chiefly from Canada. Exports and imports of other types of wood are small, the imports consisting of tropical and other special types for non-essential uses.

The known mineral resources of the United States far surpass those of any other comparable area of the world. Of the eighteen major metals, the U.S. ranks first in the production of eight; and together with the British Empire controls over two-thirds of the

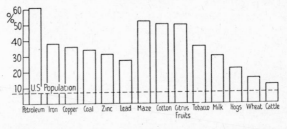

8. The U.S.A. proportion of world output of important agricultural and mineral products 1937. The U.S.A. has about 7% of the world's population and area.

total mineral output of the world, including a high proportion of each essential mineral. There are undeveloped areas in South America and Africa and the U.S.S.R. which may possess great mineral resources; but for the next decade or so the power of coal, iron, petroleum, and copper will contribute more to the strength of the American economy than to that of any other conceivable political unit.

The proportions of world output for which the United States was responsible in 1937 are shown in Graph 8. In this year American mines and wells were operating well below capacity. Nevertheless, of the four major mineral and fuel products,

IV. NATURAL PRODUCTS

1. OIL-FIELDS (*Fairchild Aerial Surveys, Inc.*)

2. COPPER MINES (*Alfred T. Palmer, from "Fortune"*)

they produced 38% of the world's iron, 37% of its copper, 34% of its coal, and 62% of its petroleum. They also produced 30% of the world's lead and zinc, supplies of aluminium, sulphur, phosphate, and potash sufficient for American use, and gold and silver in quantities for which no use exists. The only important shortages were of nickel, tin, mercury, and some of the steel alloys—manganese, chromium, antimony, and tungsten. The war-time problem presented by these shortages will be discussed later in the chapter on the War Industries.

Minerals and fuels are of vital importance in modern industry, and a major source of American strength, but the total number of people engaged in extracting them is small. The proportion of the employed population engaged in mining increased steadily from almost nothing at the beginning of the nineteenth century to a peak of 2·6% in the decade 1910–20. The proportion fell slightly during the 1920's for the same reasons that the proportion in manufacturing industry fell—a shift in demand from things to services, coupled with increased efficiency in the production of things. The depression has accentuated the fall, since mining contributes largely to the capital-goods industries, and in 1935 it was estimated that the proportion in mining of persons actually at work was less than 2%.

Although American mines produce a very large proportion of the world's supplies of minerals and fuels, these are not normally exported in quantity; American industry consumes similar proportions. In most cases, however, production could be expanded well above present levels and a surplus made available to meet exceptional domestic or export demands. Coal production since the World War has fluctuated between 400 and 600 million tons; but it has been as depressed as the British coal industry, and could expand output to at least 700 million tons. The practical capacity of the pig-iron industry is about 45 million tons, which is well above the output of recent years. The bar on Graph 8 represents a 1937 output of about 37 million tons. Domestic iron ore and scrap could, if necessary, provide the whole of its requirements for capacity production. The copper mines have suffered severely in the last decade from the depression and the loss of export markets; their output in 1929, while less than capacity, was 56% greater than the 1935–39 average and 20% greater than in 1937. Even in the case of petroleum a considerable expansion of output would be possible if present schemes designed to limit production were suspended and new drilling intensified. Some idea of what might be possible can be gained from the experience of the last war, when the production of minerals was expanded by something like 25% above the levels of 1913–14, which were relatively prosperous years. A great expansion of production occurred during the prosperous '20's despite stationary employment figures, and the 1929 output was a third higher than the wartime peak. Actual production has since been much lower, but capacity has not been much affected, and there is no doubt that it could be raised in case of necessity above the 1929 figures.

The principal raw fuels, in addition to coal and petroleum, are natural gas and water-power. Natural gas is a by-product of the petroleum industry, and is extensively used only in the United States. It is piped for hundreds of miles from the wells to industrial centres, where it makes an ideal fuel for domestic and industrial uses. America is not particularly well endowed with potential water power compared with some other countries, although much better endowed than either Britain or Germany. But many dams have been constructed since the World War, and water now provides about 8% of the nation's total supply of power.

Even in the depression decade there have been the spectacular developments at Boulder Dam [1] and on the Tennessee and Columbia Rivers.   Further development will probably not be rapid, because most of the potential power at present unutilized is in regions remote from present markets. It is, in any case, unnecessary to do so, since the present supply of fuels together with the unutilized capacity of coal mines and oil wells could provide more raw fuel than existing plants could possibly consume.

[1] See Plate VIII, p. 89.

CHAPTER III

MANUFACTURING INDUSTRY

THE most remarkable fact about American manufacturing industry is its productivity. The number
of persons employed in it is less than twice the
number similarly employed in Great Britain, but the
total output is several times as great.

It is possible to compare productivity per person
employed in different countries, as we did in the case
of agriculture, by valuing both products and the raw
materials used in making them at the same prices for
all countries. " Value added by manufacture " is the
difference between the value of the products and that
of the raw materials, and this divided by the number
of persons engaged (wage-earners, salaried employees,
and employers) gives us an index of industrial productivity per head. In the United States in 1935
value added by manufacture amounted to about £430
per person engaged in manufacturing industry (including construction and mining). In Great Britain it
amounted to less than £180. Accurate figures for
other countries are not obtainable, but it is probable
that Great Britain is, in this respect, representative
of most other manufacturing countries. The Canadian
figure would probably be much the same as the
American, and New Zealand's not much lower ; but
the Australian is slightly lower than the British, and the
same is probably true of the manufacturing countries
of Western Europe, with the possible exception of
Norway and Sweden.

This comparison somewhat exaggerates the difference

between the efficiency of American and British industry: it measures value added by manufacture per
person directly engaged, without making allowance for
persons indirectly engaged, *e.g.*, in making the capital
goods which are being used up, and in supplying
various legal, accounting, postal and other services.
Payments to this " indirect " labour amount to about
one-third the total value added by manufacture in the
United States, and to a much lower proportion in
England, where complete figures are not available.
But it is obvious that an adjustment for this factor could
not reduce productivity per head in American manufacturing to less than double the British level.

This is a striking conclusion, but there can be no
doubt that it is correct. Wherever it is possible to
measure directly in physical units the output of
industry in the two countries, as it is in coal-mining,
steel, flour, tin plate, etc., this marked disparity is
found, the American workman producing from a
fraction more to four times as much as the British.
Further confirmation is provided by the average wages
in manufacturing industry (Graph 5, p. 22).

The reasons for the superior efficiency of American
industry have been mentioned briefly in the first
chapter; although it must be admitted that no
entirely satisfactory explanation has ever been given.
Here we shall ignore the more fundamental " non-
economic " factors, although these have doubtless
been of some importance, and concentrate on three
immediate causes: the first is the greater amount of
capital in the form of machines and energy which
the American worker has at his disposal; the second,
which is distinct though not unrelated, the larger scale
of American production; and the third, the technical
progress of recent years, which has been more pronounced in America than in Europe.

The extent to which the machine increases the output

of labour varies a great deal from industry to industry. It has been found least effective in the production of furniture and clothing; in numerous other lines it has increased the efficiency of labour tenfold and more. Much also depends upon the type of machine. Motor-cars were produced by machine methods from the first, but the introduction of the moving assembly line resulted in a further marked increase in output per workman. Much of the increase in efficiency of American labour since the beginning of the century, which is estimated at something like 250%, and much of the superiority of American manufacturing efficiency over that elsewhere, can be accounted for by the fact that machine methods are more generally used in America now than ever before or in any other country, and that the machines used are, in general, more elaborate and intricate.

It is more difficult to measure capital than any of the other quantities with which we have been dealing. The best we can do is (1) to estimate the total value of tools, machines, and factories, making allowance for changes in prices; and (2) to estimate the mechanical energy consumed by the machines. It is clear that these two measures need not give the same result. Normally one would expect them to increase or decrease together, but there are some quite intricate tools which use no mechanical power, and the ratio of capital value to power varies greatly from one type of machine to another. Graph 10 (p. 54) shows that the value of capital used in American manufacturing industry and the amount of power consumed have followed very different courses.

The accumulation of capital in Western countries during the last century has passed through several fairly well-defined stages. In the first, in the case of new countries, farms are equipped with buildings and stock; this is what was happening in America up

to the Civil War.   In the second the railways are built;
this stage, in America, lasted until about 1890.   In
the third stage industry is equipped with factories,
tools, and machines; Graph 10 shows that this was
accomplished with remarkable speed between 1890
and 1920.   In the fourth, represented in America by
the 1920's, new capital investment takes the form of
residential and commercial buildings, " public utility "
plants, highways, and other public works.   The 1930's,
in America, have been so depressed that almost no
new private investment has been undertaken.

Graph 10, curve (A), traces the accumulation of
capital in manufacturing industry, which has increased
something like fourfold since 1890.   Almost the whole
of the increase, however, occurred before 1920.   Since
then industrial progress has assumed new forms.

Curve (B) traces the changes in the capacity of
industry's " prime movers "—steam, internal com-
bustion, and electric.   This capacity has increased
steadily since the first Census of Manufacturing in
1879;   and the increase since 1919 has been at an
accelerated rate.   Graph 9 shows that over half the
energy consumed in the world is consumed in the
United States; on a *per capita* basis consumption in the
United States is almost four times as great as in Great
Britain and almost six times as great as in Germany.
This is partly due to the fact that one person in five
in the United States possesses a high-powered motor-
car, and uses it extensively.   But mechanical energy
is also more widely used in manufacturing, where
horsepower per worker is about twice what it is in
Britain.   The increase in the use of power in America
has been marked in all branches of industry; since
1899 its use in textiles increased by 78%, in iron and
steel by 158%, and in non-ferrous metals and chemicals
by over 250%.   At the same time the type of power
used has changed;   over half the total capacity of

V. EXTREMES OF MODERN MANU-FACTURING

1. HAND WORKER IN MACHINE TOOL INDUSTRY

(Dmitri Kessel, from "Fortune")

2. MASS PRODUCTION: CORRIDOR IN FORD'S RIVER ROUGE MOTOR WORKS

(Charles Sheeler, courtesy of Worcester Art Museum and "Fortune")

prime movers is now supplied by electric motors, which are much more effective than steam for many kinds of industrial operations.

Closely related to the extensive use of machines and power is the second factor accounting for the high productivity of American manufacturing industry; viz., the large scale of operations. Machinery and mechanical power cannot be used economically where

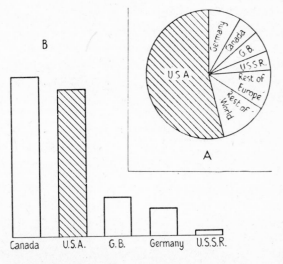

9. Consumption of energy from coal, oil, gas, and water-power 1937–39. (A) shows the proportion of total consumption in different countries and areas. (B) shows energy consumption per head of the population.

production is on a small scale; some of the most productive types of machinery, such as the conveyor belt, cannot be used economically except where the scale of production is enormous. The huge internal American market, almost entirely free from obstacles to inter-state and inter-regional trade, has made possible the development of large-scale production; and the possibility of large-scale production, coupled with the availability of capital, has resulted in the extensive use of the most effective types of machine.

This is true only as a general principle. Small-scale industry has survived in the production of many things in the United States, as elsewhere. Where the economies resulting from using capital on a large scale are not present, or small, as in textiles and shoes, there is seldom enough to be gained from a large output to offset the " diseconomies " of bureaucratic management. Moreover, many industries are un-suited to mass production, either because the total demand for their output is small, which was the case with airplanes before the war, or because each product is specific, and made to order, as in the machine tool industry. The average size of industrial plants of all kinds in the United States has apparently not increased substantially since the World War.

What is significant, however, is that the great increases in productivity in recent years have occurred precisely in those industries where the size of the plant has increased substantially—the industries in which machinery effective for large-scale production has been perfected. By far the largest increases in scale occurred in the production of motor-cars and tyres, where the number of wage-earners per plant more than trebled between 1914 and 1929; and these industries also showed far the greatest gains in productivity per man-hour—between 200% and 300%. Substantial in-creases in scale—between 25% and 50%—took place in petroleum refining, steel, blast-furnaces, meat-packing, and paper and pulp manufacture, and the gains in productivity in these industries ranged from 30% to 150%. The only important exception to the rule was cement manufacture, which showed large gains in productivity despite a small decrease in the average size of plant.

When an industry, like the motor-car industry

expands, the economies which result are only partly due to the large scale of operations which it makes possible in individual plants. There are further economies resulting from the large scale of the industry, which are more or less independent of any changes in the size of plants. These include the utilization of by-products, the development of efficient subsidiary industries, and the co-operative subsidizing of research. But the most important is the specialization which it permits within the industry. When the total output is small, all the operations tend to be performed in a single plant, or under a single management. When the output is large, individual companies and plants can specialize on one particular kind or part of the product; with gains analogous to those achieved by Adam Smith's makers of pins. A striking example is found in the motor-car industry, where the manufacture of many parts is carried on by specialized firms, where the manufacture of bodies has become an industry distinct from that turning out the final product, and where each manufacturer of cars concentrates on a few similar types. This division of function is somewhat obscured by the fact that many plants of diverse types are sometimes united under " holding companies "—Chevrolet, Buick, Cadillac, the Fisher Body Company, and other units of the industry are owned and controlled by General Motors—but such aggregations can, and sometimes do, give the industry the best of both worlds. For manufacturing purposes the individual plants are almost completely autonomous, so that specialization of function is not interfered with. On the other hand, things which can most effectively be done co-operatively, like the maintenance of research, are undertaken by the parent body. This is true at least of many holding companies in manufacturing industry, which thus serve a useful functional purpose; it has not been true, in general, of the " public utility " holding companies (*e.g.*, in electric power) which in many cases serve no useful function, and have been created to expedite financial manipulations and to " milk " the operating companies by levying excessive charges for certain " services ".

The third factor which is mainly responsible for the high productivity of American industry is advancing technique. Prior to 1920 little was spent on industrial research, which was generally considered, as it is still in this country, a sort of unnecessary luxury. Since then the number of full-time researchers employed by industry has increased from 8,000 to 42,000, and expenditure on industrial research is now about £50,000,000 each year—which is forty times the annual budget of the colleges and University of Oxford. The largest employers of researchers are, as one might expect, the chemical and petroleum industries, but there are few important industries which employ less than 1,000. Their most spectacular accomplishments have been the development of new products—artificial silks and rubbers, static-less radio, technicolour television—but much more important have been the steady improvements in the efficiency of more ordinary things. Since 1920 they have increased the number of electric units secured from a pound of coal by 115%, the amount of tractive effort from a gallon of petrol by 200%, the amount of light from a unit of electricity by 55%, and the efficiency of lubricating oil by 85% over that of the best natural product. The list could be extended to almost any length. In the nineteenth century American industry imported its methods from Europe. Today it still does, to a certain extent, but it exports far more in the way of new products and new processes than it imports.

There have also been advances which have little to do with scientific research in the narrower sense. Frederick " Speedy " Taylor showed the American steel industry how to cut its labour costs by Stakhanovist methods long before the idea occurred to Stalin; he has had almost as many imitators as there have been American industrial managers. Standardization has resulted in large savings; Herbert Hoover's Department of Commerce officially sponsored it in the 1920's, and persuaded industry drastically to reduce the number

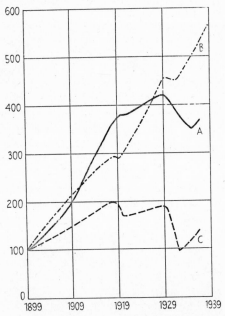

10. The changing character of American manufacturing industry. (A) shows total value of capital employed, (B) total energy consumed, and (C) total labour employed, measured in man-hours.

of types and sizes of dozens of products from paving bricks to range boilers. Business management has been elevated to something approaching professional status in the United States, although the justification and consequences of this are still in dispute. Universities include it in their curriculum on a par with languages, history, mathematics, and the natural sciences (Harvard has a large and successful postgraduate school devoted entirely to its study), and thousands of would-be business men devote several preliminary years to mastering the principles of production, marketing, finance, and advertising.

The joint effect of capital, energy, size, and technical progress on the productivity of American industry is suggested by a comparison of Graphs 10 and 11.

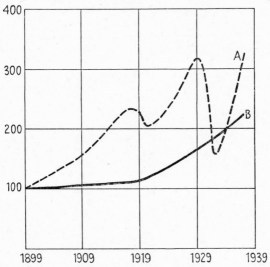

11. (A) Physical volume of production, and (B) production per labour-hour in American manufacturing industry.

Curve (A) of Graph 11 traces the total output of manufacturing industry, measured by "value added by manufacture". Its general course has been upward, although the two great depressions since the World War caused violent fluctuations. Curve (B) of Graph 11 traces output per labour-hour, which is the best possible measure of industrial productivity: its course has been steadily upward, and its level is now two and a half times what it was in 1900.

In interpreting these facts it is necessary to distinguish sharply between the period up to 1920 and the one since 1920. Prior to 1920 American industry was equipping itself with capital: the curves of capital value and of energy on Graph 10 were rising at more or less equal rates, and employment (curve C) was increasing too, but not as rapidly. The gain in productivity in this period can be ascribed almost wholly to the increase in capital (and energy) per head, and to economies resulting from the larger scale of plants and industries.

After 1920 the amount of capital per head increased very little while employment fell, and the gain in productivity which has occurred must be accounted for in other ways. Increases in the size of plants and industries had something to do with it, as we have seen. But the most important factors have undoubtedly been the increased use of mechanical energy, which has accelerated since 1920, and the improvements in machines, and the technique of using them, which cannot be shown in a single graph. The future progress of American industry would seem to lie with the researcher, rather than the investor.

Steel has long been the "giant" of American industry. In the railway age, and the later period when industry was building its plant, its position was unchallenged; and the industries engaged in the production of iron and its products still account for about 30% of the total output of manufactured goods. The great iron-ore region is in northern Minnesota, and the ore is shipped through the Great Lakes on a fleet of vessels nearly as large as the merchant navy of France to the great blast-furnaces of the Eastern States (Plate VI). The capacity of the American steel industry is almost as great as that of all the rest of the world, although actual production during the depression of the 1930's has been considerably less.

Another 13% of the total "value added by manufacture" consists of the non-ferrous metals, lumber, stone, clay, glass, and their products. Some of these are rapidly gaining in importance, notably aluminium and the plastics, which promise to supplant steel in many of its uses if the airplane age becomes a reality. The other 57% of American manufactures are non-durable: food, drink, tobacco, textiles, rubber and leather products, chemicals, mineral fuels, paper and printing, all of which are produced in about the same proportions as in England.

Classification by particular industries is difficult, because the increasing specialization of function has blurred the customary divisions based on final product. It is roughly true, however, that the six most important industries, all of comparable size, account for more than a third of the total value added by manufacture. The most important of these is motor-cars, bodies and parts, and printing and publishing is a close second. The other four, in order of size, are machinery (foundries and shops), steel works and blast-furnaces, clothing, and electrical machinery and apparatus. The preponderance of the industries producing motor-cars and machinery is again striking, and illustrates forcibly the most distinctive feature of American manufacturing.

The construction industry has not achieved the same economies of large-scale production that have marked the development of many branches of manufacture. It is still predominantly, as in this country, carried on by numerous small contractors. About two and one-half million persons were engaged in it in 1930, at the end of a decade of great constructional activity; since then it has been extremely depressed. It is not an efficient industry, if we measure its product in terms of money or labour cost, but it has solved one problem much more successfully than construction industries in other countries, that of speed. Large numbers of

VI. IRON ORE COMES BY THE GREAT LAKES

1. THE START: DULUTH HARBOUR (*Mondiale*)

2. THE FINISH: STEEL WORKS IN THE EAST (*Ewing Galloway*)

men, efficiently organized and co-ordinated, are employed on single projects, and buildings are completed in a fraction of the time ordinarily required in England. The main unit of Radio City is far larger than any building outside America; it was completed in 16 months from the time the ground was broken. The steel construction of the Time and Life building, a 34-story unit of Radio City, required only 44 working days. Large factories are completed and put in operation within a few months of the time that plans are approved. This fact is of the greatest relevance to the problems which we shall consider in the next chapter: in a country turning over to a war economy speed of construction is far more important than cheapness.

CHAPTER IV

WAR INDUSTRIES

IN the long run the division between war industries
and peace industries has little meaning; if time is
available for transferring resources, all industry can
be utilized in the production of things essential for the
prosecution of war. Economic strength in the general
sense in which we have been discussing it, the power to
produce goods and services, is therefore in these circumstances a fairly accurate measure of economic
strength for waging war. Much will of course depend
upon the efficiency of the Government which directs
the transfer and upon the adaptability of labour;
something will depend upon the precise type of production being carried on in peace-time. It may also
be the case that a strong peace-time economy will be
handicapped in waging war by shortages of certain vital
raw materials which the war makes inaccessible. But
the proposition that in the long run general economic
strength is the equivalent of war potential is so near to
the whole truth that we should not be justified in
devoting a chapter to discussing the modifications.

In the very short run, on the other hand, general
economic strength is almost irrelevant. What matters
is the immediately available supply of arms and
munitions and men trained to use them. The states-
men and statisticians who argued that the French and
British Empires could not be defeated by Germany
because their national incomes and financial resources
were so much greater, overlooked this vital fact. The
French Empire has been defeated; and the British
Empire has not been, in the words of the Prime Minister, because of the few to whom so many owe so much.

He was referring to the R.A.F., and it is true that few others mattered in the critical months after Dunkirk.

In the long run the United States possesses by far the greatest military potential of any nation, one which is probably equal to the combined military potential of the whole of Europe. In the short run it possesses one of the weakest. Its navy is formidable, but its army and air force are almost negligible. With the exception of the military plane industry, of very recent development and relatively small size, and the naval dockyards, it possesses no war industries worthy of the name—no munitions industry, no private industry producing guns, military rifles, or tanks.

In this chapter we shall be concerned primarily neither with the long run nor with the short, but with the much more interesting intermediate period, ranging from a few months to a few years, in which it should be possible, given vigorous and intelligent direction from the Government, to transfer a major portion of the resources in certain specially relevant industries to war production. The most important of these are the industries now producing steel and minor metals, motor-cars, airplanes, ships, and chemicals. In addition we must examine the supplies to these industries of their essential factors of production: skilled labour, machine tools, raw materials, and power.

The difficulties of transforming a peace-time economy to war production are very great, and in the case of America there is an unfortunate tendency to underestimate them. The comparison with the American position in 1917, or the British position in recent years, is misleading. America in 1917 had been supplying the Allies with armaments and munitions of all sorts, orders for which had been placed on a large scale from the first months of the war. As a result she entered the war with a sizeable munitions industry, and her task was the relatively simple one of expanding existing capacity. Britain found herself in a deplorable state of disarmament when the Nazi threat became menacing. But she had an armaments industry—firms like Vickers, which, though they had been producing on a small scale, possessed the capacity and the experience which made rapid expansion possible. America is almost literally starting from scratch. The plants which produced military explosives, small arms, and guns during the World War have all been scrapped or converted to other purposes. The Allies, prior to the collapse of France, had not placed orders on the scale of 1914–17; indeed, apart from military airplanes they had ordered almost no armaments or munitions of any sort. This was partly because they were better equipped themselves than they had been in 1914, partly because they were unable to borrow dollars. The result was that before the middle of 1940 only the first preliminary steps had been taken. America's position is comparable to that of Germany in 1933, and it took the Germans, with singleness of purpose and authoritarian powers, five years to achieve quantity production. America is now aroused, and the National Defense Advisory Commission (N.D.A.C.) is setting about its task of organizing industry with great vigour, but there are difficulties and bottle-necks, which only time can overcome. The N.D.A.C. hopes to equip an Army of 1,200,000 and supply 35,000 'planes by the middle of 1942, and to complete a two-ocean Navy by 1944.

Steel and motor-cars are the two great basic industries which would be called upon to provide the bulk of American armament requirements: it is significant that the two leading members of the N.D.A.C.—William Knudsen and Edward Stettinius— have been borrowed from General Motors and U.S. Steel. Both industries have enormous capacity measured by European standards. The steel industry has four times the capacity of the British and more than double the capacity of the German. It would, in time of war, produce the guns and shells, the armour plating for the ships, and the most essential material for tanks, engines, instruments, and small arms. It is now rapidly expanding its " bottlenecks "—electric furnaces to make the highest grade steel, and armour-plate capacity. The motor-car industry is, both relatively and absolutely, still larger. In 1937 Great Britain produced about 500,000 motor-cars, the British Dominions 200,000, and Germany 340,000; the United States alone produced 4,800,000. Every six months the American industry runs off the assembly lines as many cars as exist in the United Kingdom. These comparisons, striking as they are, under-state the size of the American industry, because the average American car is larger, heavier, and more powerful that that produced in any other country; its horse-power, by the standard English rating, is thirty. The importance of the plant and skilled labour attached to this industry in equipping a mechanized army and an air force cannot be over-estimated. They can quickly turn out the transport vehicles which will be required. With some adaptation and new tools they can produce tanks, guns, ammunition, aero-engines, and motor torpedo boats on a scale no other country can equal.

The difficulty in both cases is time. The great Bethlehem and Midvale Steel plants which constituted America's World War armaments industry had been scrapped. In time of peace the American army relies chiefly on its own small arsenals. The War Department has from time to time placed " educational orders " with some private firms, but these have been on a pathetically small scale. Almost all the great mass production corporations have now been awarded contracts for war materials, but they will have to learn the business, and then equip their plants, before they can fill the orders.

The easiest production problems are explosives, shells, and small arms. During the World War du Pont supplied 40% of all Allied explosives; and although its plants were converted to other uses after the war, America, as a result of the World War, has a large chemical industry, and new powder plants are easy to erect. New du Pont and Hercules plants will be ready in 1941, and sixteen others are planned with a total capacity well in excess of World War peak production. Shells can be turned out in any quantity by the steel and other metal industries: the only bottleneck here is machine tools. The companies now producing sporting rifles—Remington, which produced a million rifles in twelve months in 1918, Winchester, and Savage—could solve the problem of volume production of the U.S. Army's new automatic rifle, the Garand, and other small arms in from one to two years' time. General Motors will be producing machine guns in quantity by 1942.

The most difficult production problems are heavy artillery, precision instruments, tanks (especially heavy tanks), warships, and airplanes and motors. It requires a year to build a plant to make big guns, and from a year to eighteen months more to make the guns. As in the last war the job is being entrusted to the Bethlehem and Midvale plants. Precision instruments are technically the trickiest job of all, and the short run situation would be desperate had not the last war, by shutting off German supplies, created an American optical industry. Light and medium tanks can be produced by the motor-car industry and by other firms which have filled educational orders. Chrysler is building a large arsenal for "mediums," and will be producing in about a year. No firm has had any experience in producing heavy tanks because the Army, prior to the invasion of France, considered them impracticable. Orders have now been placed

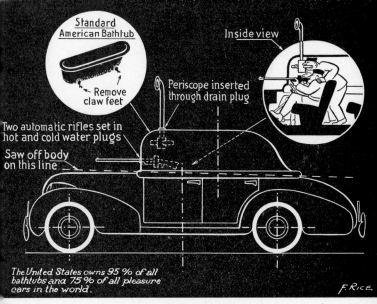

Standard American Bathtub

→ Remove claw feet

Inside view

Periscope inserted through drain plug

Two automatic rifles set in hot and cold water plugs

Saw off body on this line

The United States owns 95% of all bathtubs and 75% of all pleasure cars in the world.

F. RICE

VII. AID FOR BRITAIN

I. AIRPLANE FACTORY (*Paul Popper*)

2. HOW THE U.S.A. CAN CONTRIBUTE IMMEDIATELY TO BRITAIN'S WAR EFFORT!
(*New Yorker*)

E (U.S.A. 2)

with the great Baldwin Locomotive Works. America is much better equipped for sea than for land warfare; the American Navy, about the size of the British at the outbreak of war, and merchant marine—9,000,000 gross tons, in addition to 2,500,000 on the Great Lakes, which is about half the size of the British—are both much larger than in 1914. The capacity of the American shipbuilding industry is not much smaller than the British.

Present plans call for a 70% increase in the Navy, by 1944 or 1945. The Navy has eight yards, all clogged with new construction, and there are seven private yards capable of building warships. It is probable that the building programme will be expanded, but the results will not be evident in our " intermediate " period. Armour plate is supplied by one naval plant and three private steel companies; capacity has been doubled in the past year, and will have to be doubled again if the present programme is to be completed on time. What the American naval dockyards can accomplish when pressed is suggested by their record in the last war, when almost 200 destroyers were completed between 1918 and 1920. Fifty of these were recently transferred to Britain.

It was during the last war that commercial ship-building attained the status of a large-scale industry. In its effort to build a " bridge of ships " to Europe, the United States Shipbuilding Corporation completed over 3,000,000 tons of shipping in a single year, and 9,000,000 tons in all. Quality was sacrificed to speed, and the American merchant marine still consists very largely of the inferior obsolete ships built at this time. Since 1938 the new Federal Maritime Commission has been carrying out an extensive programme of building modern ships. The total commercial tonnage completed in 1939 was 300,000, in 1940 about 500,000. Although the expansion of ship-building facilities is a very slow job, and there is a shortage of skilled labour, it is thought that the shipyards now in service could produce 1,000,000 tons by 1942. Britain's peak production (in 1918) was 1,350,000 tons, a figure which she is having difficulty in reaching at present. The building and reconditioning of ways in yards on the Atlantic, the Pacific, and the Gulf of Mexico should approximately double American capacity.

The producers of military airplanes comprise the only other American war industry of any size; and it is new and small compared with the German and British industries. During the World War America produced 18,000 'planes and 40,000 motors, starting from scratch. After 1919 production was on a very small scale, and almost wholly commerical, until 1939. The capacity in 1940 was about 10,000 or 12,000 a year, of all types. There were forty-five 'plane companies employing about 100,000 men. To attain President Roosevelt's output of 50,000 'planes per year they will have to invest about $500,000,000 in plant and employ almost 400,000 additional workers. This would normally take three or four years, and the N.D.A.C. estimates that the January 1941 output of 1,000 military 'planes cannot be expanded to 3,000 per month before April 1942.

Many of the estimates of American output which have appeared in the Press have been wildly exaggerated; where they have not been dishonest they have hopelessly confused the potential and the actual. Americans build plants rapidly, but even in California, where the bulk of the industry is located, they must be built. The superiority of American industry is most marked in the field of mass production, and planes are not yet mass produced. Total output has been too small, and technical progress has in the past been so rapid that the tooling of equipment for mass production has not been worth while. The Burbank, California, plant of

a General Motors company has shown that the moving
assembly line which revolutionized the motor-car industry is practicable in 'plane production; but a
minimum of four months is required to get the line
going, and a further six months to produce the first
'plane. In almost any ten months in recent years the
original designs would have become obsolete. The
character of the industry is strikingly revealed by
figures of the amount of capital employed: the
Chevrolet plant (motor-cars) uses $2,600 per worker;
Glenn Martin, one of the leading airplane producers,
$800.

With unlimited official assistance, or under compulsion, the industry could probably shorten the estimated
three- or four-year period required to expand output
to 50,000 planes. But there are three bottlenecks:
skilled labour, machine tools, and engines. The first of
these is the least important: the necessary skill can be
acquired in a few months, and a reduction in motor-car
output could easily free sufficient semi-skilled labour.
Machine tools—*i.e.*, tools and machines to make the
necessary machinery—are vital in making planes,
engines, and numerous other war supplies as well.
They constitute a general bottleneck, and the industry
producing them is discussed below. Engines have so
far proved the great disappointment of American
production.

It would appear at first sight as if the motor-car industry, which turns out almost 5,000,000 engines a
year, could easily supply the 100,000 or so required for
50,000 planes. Unfortunately, however, the motor-car
industry has had little experience in the manufacture
of the very high-powered engines used in modern
military planes, and the plane companies have so far
relied on two specialized producers—Pratt and Whitney,
and Wright—whose present capacity is about 18,000.
By the middle of 1941 they hope to more than double

this figure, and Ford will be producing by 1942; but their engines are all air-cooled, and liquid-cooled motors are preferable from the point of view of stream-lining. Although a number of American companies have been experimenting with liquid-cooled motors, the only plant producing them is the Allison division of General Motors, whose products at present are few, new, and untried, and probably will not exceed 500 a month before the middle of 1941. The abortive negotiations with the Ford Company to manufacture Rolls Royce engines (liquid cooled), a task subsequently assumed by the Packard Company, were intended to fill this important gap. It will probably be filled in 1942, but certainly not sooner.

Behind the war industries are the essential resources of production—skilled labour, power, machines, and raw materials. Deficiencies of the first two of these are not likely to be serious. Labour has lost much of its skill in a decade of depression, and never possessed some of the skill now required of it, but except in a few special industries—precision instruments, machine tools —it can be quickly trained. Not much skill is required on an assembly line. The supply of power is probably sufficient: there has been a good deal of political controversy about its adequacy recently, and the N.D.A.C. has been urging Congress to expand the capacity of the Tennessee Valley Authority's plants (see Chapter V). But the total American output of power is so great that it is inconceivable that sufficient cannot be made available to the munitions industries by economies in other directions.

The various plants engaged in making machinery account for about 12% of the total capacity of American industry—an extremely high proportion. The machine tool industry proper, which supplies tools for chipping, grinding, cutting, and gauging, consists of 250 small units, chiefly in New England and the North-east, whose aggregate gross output, although the largest in the world, rarely approaches £100,000,000 a year. The industry had a military origin, for it came into existence to tool the early rifles, then the most exacting mechanism to manufacture in the whole of industry. The vast majority of its products are now, of course, for non-military use, but the increasing mechanization of modern armies has made it a basic military industry of vital importance. It is what the Americans call a "feast or famine" industry, because the demand for its products, which are capital goods to make capital goods, fluctuate violently with the trade cycle. At the present moment it is feasting, with a tremendous military demand added to a moderate commercial one. Much of its production has always been for export; and even Great Britain has relied on it to a considerable extent, and increasingly since the beginning of the war, for its machine tools, importing, with France, $65,000,000 worth in 1939. It is not and cannot be made a mass production industry, because most machines have to be built to specification. Much of the work must be done by hand, and the labour employed must be highly trained and highly skilled.[1]

Because it requires highly skilled labour, it is not easy to expand capacity. The only solution, in the short run, is to divert production from other purposes, *e.g.*, the export trade and motor-car manufacture, to production for the airplane and other war industries. The tool manufacturers have promised the N.D.A.C. priority on national defence orders, but other important steps, which might include a ban on exports to certain countries and on new motor-car models next year, have not yet been taken.

Is there any danger that American production will be held up by shortages of essential raw materials? The answer depends to a certain extent on the circumstances

[1] See Plate V, p. 49.

in which America finds herself engaged in war, since these will determine her ability to import. We shall return to this question in Chapter VII. Here we shall make the worst reasonable assumption; viz., that imports are cut off altogether except from other American countries.

There would in these circumstances be a few serious shortages, and a number which would be less serious. Some time ago the War Department drew up a list of " critical " and " strategic " materials in short supply, but little was done about them until June 1940, when the Reconstruction Finance Corporation (see pp. 87–8) was authorized to build stockpiles, on which it is planning to spend over £100,000,000. Among the less serious shortages are wool, silk, mercury, aluminium, and toluol (needed for T.N.T.). Cotton and rayon can be substituted for wool and silk for most purposes (*e.g.*, rayon for silk in parachutes) and large economies are possible in the field of luxury consumption. Mercury is produced on a small scale, and there are low grade ores which could be exploited. The supply of aluminium is not very short, and there are alternative sources in the Western hemisphere. A method has been devised for securing toluol as a by-product in the manufacture of high-octane petrol. The really serious problems are presented by rubber, tin, and the vital ferro-alloys—viz., nickel, tungsten, chromium, antimony, and especially manganese, without which steel cannot be made.

The United States imports half a million tons of rubber a year—about half the world's production—from British Malaya and the Netherlands East Indies, and while substantial economies in its use would be possible in time of war, special war demands would be heavy. The possible solutions are two: the purchase of large stocks while trade with the Far East is still free from interference, and the production of synthetic

rubber.   Both alternatives have been adopted.   Cotton
has been traded to Britain for rubber, and further large
purchases for stocks were made by the U.S. Government
last summer.   The only problems of synthetic supply
are financial and economic; various alternative processes have been developed which produce technically
satisfactory substitutes from coal, oil, gas, vegetables,
and grains.   The cost is at present about 50% higher
than that of natural rubber.   The N.D.A.C. has
authorized the erection of plants which in eighteen
months will be ready to produce about 100,000 tons
annually.

Tin is also imported chiefly from British Malaya and
the Netherlands East Indies.   Here, too, large economies would be possible in war-time.   Thirty per cent.
of requirements could be met from scrap.   Half the
present consumption is in the manufacture of tinplate,
for which substitutes could be used.   An alternative
source of supply is Bolivia, and although neither Bolivia
nor the United States possesses plants for smelting tin,
other smelting plants could easily and quickly be converted for this purpose.   To meet any short run
difficulties the Government last summer purchased for
stock the equivalent of a year's supplies, but deliveries
will not be completed before the middle of 1941.

Nickel is only nominally in short supply.   Ninety per
cent. of the world supply comes from Canada, and
circumstances in which this source would cease to be
available are almost inconceivable.   The other four
important ferro-alloys in short supply—manganese,
chromium, tungsten, and antimony—exist in the
United States, and at high cost up to 50% of requirements could be domestically produced.   The case of
manganese is particularly serious: over 1,500,000 tons
annually will be required (double the peace-time consumption) and little over half this quantity can be
produced domestically or elsewhere in the Western

Hemisphere. In the case of most ferro-alloys there is no solution possible if overseas trade is cut off, except acquisition of stocks, which is proceeding, and the increased use of substitute metals where these exist.

It was Hindenburg who said after the last war: " The brilliant, if pitiless, war industry (of America) had entered the service of patriotism and had not failed it. . . . They understood war." Doubtless it will be possible for someone to say the same thing again, but not this year. The N.D.A.C. has not yet, as the War Industries Board had in 1918, the power to impose priorities or commandeer plant; and the steel and airplane manufacturers have behaved " reasonably " rather than patriotically in insisting on satisfactory excess profits and amortization laws before proceeding with their expansion programmes. These difficulties are temporary—they will, like the technical bottlenecks, be overcome—but it would be both unreasonable and imprudent to expect too much too soon.

CHAPTER V

DEPRESSION AND NEW DEAL

THE economic and social legislation for which President Roosevelt and his party have been responsible during the past eight years has had two aims: recovery from the most severe depression any modern industrial country has ever experienced; and the introduction of certain reforms in American economic organization. The eloquent speeches of President Roosevelt and his lieutenants, the extraordinary resentment which certain of his measures have provoked in the business community, and the great publicity which they have been given in the world press, have undoubtedly caused many people, both in America and outside it, to form an exaggerated opinion of the importance of the New Deal in re-fashioning American economic life. American economic life today does differ in important respects from American economic life in 1929; but the depression has had as much to do with the change as has the New Deal.

The New Deal programme consisted of a number of specific measures designed to achieve recovery with reform. We shall consider below how effective these were. But the chief significance of the measures lies in the changed economic attitudes which they reflect, and which they in part caused. It is difficult to generalize, in America as in Great Britain, about public opinion on economic matters. It differs by regions, by classes, by occupations, and by individuals. But the typical economic attitude of the 1920's was certainly one of great and unjustified optimism, and of faith in the virtues of individualism and competition. Each year production and wealth were increasing: they were expected to go on increasing indefinitely. Each year the values of shares on the stock exchange rose: it was thought that there was no practicable limit to the rise. Unemployment existed, but on too small a scale to be an important national problem. Economists seriously debated whether there would ever be another slump; the man-in-the-street was sure that there would not. Some statisticians knew that the distribution of income was becoming more unequal; but while all classes and almost all occupations were increasing their incomes, relative shares seemed unimportant, and the prospect of class antagonism too remote to worry about. Widespread gambling on the stock exchange was partly responsible for the illusion that the United States was becoming a nation of capitalists.

This is, of course, a very general picture. The unemployed, and persons in depressed industries and regions, did not share the general optimism. Unemployment during the 1920's was seldom under two million. The great textile and bituminous coal industries were severely depressed. Agriculture was suffering from low prices for its basic products: thousands of banks failed in the Middle West before the depression started, and many farmers, especially in the South, were living in conditions of extreme poverty. Nevertheless most Americans in this decade had almost forgotten that economic, as opposed to commercial or technical problems, still existed.

The depression which began in the latter half of 1929 had, by the time of Roosevelt's election in 1932, completely destroyed this complacency. The market value of stock exchange securities, which had totalled $87 thousand million in 1929, was down to $19 thousand million. Physical production was down

32%, labour income 40%, construction had almost stopped, unemployment was an estimated 15 million, and there were millions of others on short time. Agricultural prices, already at a level so low as to cause acute depression, had fallen a further 60%. Bank failures, previously confined to agricultural districts, had become frequent and general throughout the country. As the day of Mr. Roosevelt's inauguration—March 4, 1933—approached they reached a climax; by the time he delivered his inaugural speech every bank in the country had been closed by decree to prevent panic-stricken runs, economic life had almost stopped, and penniless millionaires in New York were begging the price of a meal.

The realization that something was wrong with the American economy led to numerous and conflicting explanations of what was wrong. President Roosevelt's own views have not been entirely consistent, and he has changed his advisers frequently, but the vague group about him known as the New Dealers, who were responsible for most of the legislation, considered the chief evils to be the concentration of economic power and the decline in opportunities for new investment. They were not a very radical group, by European standards, for they considered both evils to be eradicable without drastic changes in the economic system, but they did foresee the danger of serious class conflicts if they were not removed. The first of these evils—the concentration of economic power—inspired most of the New Deal reform legislation; the second—the decline in opportunities for investment—the measures designed to secure recovery.

The concentration of economic power was manifested in many ways. The proportion of the occupied population employed by others—wage- and salary-earners—had risen from half in 1870 to four-fifths in 1935, and of the nine million "self-employed", two-thirds were farmers and more than half the rest retail merchants. This meant that the possibility of achieving the American frontiersman's dream of economic independence had, in most occupations, dwindled almost to vanishing point. The concentration was also reflected in the unequal distribution of income, and in the still more unequal distribution of wealth. The belief that " everyone " played the stock market during the securities boom was grossly exaggerated; according to one estimate 3% of the population owned shares in 1929, and three-tenths of 1% of the population received 78% of the dividends. It was reflected most strikingly in the growth of great corporations; in 1930 1% of the corporations owned half the wealth of all corporations, and the 200 largest had been growing so fast in the 1920's that, if they continued to grow at the same rate, they would own half the nation's wealth by 1950.

The heavy industries and some of the light ones— steel, motor-cars, chemicals, meat-packing, sugar-refining, petroleum, power, electrical equipment, and others—were dominated by a very few " oligopolies ". Their effective power to control production and restrain competition was indicated by the course of prices between 1929 and 1933: while agricultural prices were falling 63% and prices of textiles 45%, prices of agricultural implements fell only 6%, of motor-cars 16%, and of iron and steel 20%. And behind the industrial corporations, argued the New Dealers, finance played a strategic rôle, operating through holding companies and interlocking directorates which enabled skilful manipulation to multiply the power of ordinary dollars. The wide dispersal of shares (Bell Telephone had 630,000 shareholders), which seemed democratic, had the effect of rendering it impossible for any combination of shareholders to oppose auto-cratic control by directors.

The second evil, responsible for the persistence of depression and production below capacity, was the decline in opportunities for investment. There were thought to be several reasons for this: the disappearance of the frontier; the " maturity " of an economy which had already built its railways and its factories; troubled conditions in Europe which made foreign investment unattractive; and the slowing down of the rate of increase in population, which reduced the demand for dwellings and indirectly for factories and machines. During the 1920's, it was argued, special factors intervened to offset this tendency—the development of the motor-car and ancillary industries, and of electric power; the housing shortage resulting from the cessation of building during the war; and the opportunities for investment in a Europe devastated by the war. Once these special factors ceased to operate it was inevitable that employment in the capital-goods industries would decline, and with it purchasing power, prices, and production.

The New Deal was less a programme than a series of *ad hoc* legislative enactments, many of them in response to pressure from interested groups, and not all consistent with one another. But insofar as it was a programme it was designed to remove these two evils: concentration of economic power was attacked indirectly by measures designed to protect and strengthen labour and the farmer; and the decline in opportunities for investment directly by opening new ones—public or private—and by so stimulating consumption that a smaller scale of investment would be adequate to secure reasonably full employment and production. In general, the first of these designs has been accomplished with moderate success: certain reforms have been achieved, though most of them amounted to no more than England and other Western European countries accomplished years earlier. The second has met with less success: after ten years of depression over 10 million men are still unemployed, and production almost as far below capacity as when Roosevelt assumed office.

The reform programme need not be discussed in chronological order. It consisted of four types of measures: (1) " social security " legislation, designed to protect the " dispossessed " from unemployment, illness, and old age; (2) measures to strengthen independent trade unions, and thereby labour's bargaining power against capital; (3) measures to aid the farmer; and (4) legislation designed to remove certain specific evils associated with the concentration of industrial and financial power.

The nature of legislation designed to promote social security is familiar enough to readers in this country to make any detailed discussion of its principles unnecessary. The New Deal legislation borrowed heavily on Britain's experience in this field; its chief difference from the British model is that it is somewhat more cumbersome. For this the American Federal system is partly to blame: responsibility for legislation and administration is divided between the Federal Government and the States. American " individualism " is responsible for the adoption of the principle that contributions and benefits should depend upon the wage of the insured worker, which enormously complicates the bookkeeping. It is possible that, in the interests of unified control, uniformity of benefits, and the reduction of administrative expense, the whole structure of social insurance may be simplified along British lines.

The Social Security Act provided for (1) Federal old age benefits for most workers, financed by equal percentage taxes on employers and employees; (2) unemployment compensation, under State laws approved by a Social Security Board; and (3) grants to the States for maternity and child health and welfare services and assistance to the aged (*i.e.*, those not covered by the Federal benefits) and blind. The unemployment compensation is partly paid for by a Federal tax on employers, but States may supplement this from their own funds or by special taxes on employees. The grants to the States under (3) are made from general revenue; States which accept them must add an equal amount from their own revenue. Before the Act was passed Wisconsin was the only State which had an unemployment insurance system; by July 1938 every State had adopted an approved scheme. Average unemployment benefits are $10.50 (over £2) per week for a maximum period of 16 weeks, but there are wide variations between States.

The first legislation which attempted to assist labour in industrial bargaining was the National Recovery Act of 1933 (N.R.A.), the most ambitious, confused, and ineffectual of all New Deal measures. It provided for " codes of fair competition " in each industry to be drafted by the National Recovery Administration on the advice of business and labour in the industry. The nature of these codes varied greatly; in general they gave authority to business leaders to control production and prices in disregard of the anti-trust laws, recognized labour's right to organize, and fixed minimum wages and maximum hours. The N.R.A. was therefore an experiment in what has been called in England " self-government in industry ". As such it was a failure. The reduction in hours led to some increase in the number of men employed, but, as Graph 13 shows, a brief spurt in production caused by expectations of higher prices was followed by a swift relapse, and the steep rise in prices not only robbed labour of most of its gains, but convinced the public that there was much to be said for the anti-trust legislation which had been set aside. In addition, the drawing-up of the codes and their enforcement (or lack of enforcement) led to bitter recrimination. When the Supreme Court declared the act null and void its action was almost universally welcomed.

The present legislation in defence of labour is found in the Wagner Act, passed in 1935 and since amended, and the Wages and Hours Act, passed in 1938. The Wagner Act required businesses to recognize a union representing the majority of its employees, and to bargain with it; it also forbade employers to establish " company unions ", or to interfere in any other way with their employees' choice of a union. The National Labour Relations Board was set up to enforce the act. Its trickiest task is to determine in disputed cases the " appropriate unit " (*e.g.*, whether craft or industry) for collective bargaining; another of its duties is to hold elections to determine which union represents the majority of employees where this fact is contested. The Wages and Hours Act set up bodies on the lines of the British Trade Boards to fix minimum wages and maximum hours and prohibit harmful child labour. A national minimum wage of 40 cents (2 shillings) an hour for a normal maximum of 40 hours a week, with time and a half for overtime, was the eventual aim.

American trade unions have always been weak. The most important reason has been that many—perhaps most—American workers have looked upon their wage status as temporary. Another reason has been inept union leadership, a third the fierce opposition of industrial leaders, who have in general received the support of the conservative courts in fighting strikes. The change in labour attitudes resulting from the depression and the closing of opportunities for advancement to independent status, together with the Wagner Act, which has undermined the opposition of business, have given a tremendous impetus to the union movement. It has been unable to take full advantage of its opportunities because of the split between the American Federation of Labor, the association of craft unions led by William Green, and the Congress of Industrial Organizations, a new group of industrial unions organized by John Lewis; but the membership in unions has doubled since 1929 to its present figure of eight or nine millions, which represents about the same proportion of industrial labour as the British figure of four or five millions. The new labour legislation, like the National Recovery Act, has aroused bitter opposition. In particular the National Labor Relations Board is accused by business of favouritism to labour, and by the American Federation of Labor of favouritism to the Congress of Industrial Organizations. So far, however, the opposition has not been able to secure any substantial modification of the acts.

Measures to aid the farmer have been numerous, ingenious, and sometimes mutually inconsistent. Their primary aim has been to raise the prices of farm products, which had fallen much more sharply than industrial prices in the post-World War slump, and again in the depression of the 30's. Graph 12, which traces the prices of farm products since 1913, and their relation to the prices of the industrial products farmers buy (e.g., fertilizers, tractors, consumption goods), reveals the plight in which farmers found themselves when Roosevelt assumed office. The New Dealers wanted to re-establish the relation between agricultural and industrial prices which ruled before the World War, and although they have not been able to do this they have, as the graph shows, substantially improved the relation between them which existed in 1932.

The Agricultural Administration began by making " benefit payments " to farmers who agreed to reduce their acreage. This was found to be ineffective, and it has been necessary in some cases: (1) to limit crops as well as acreage, in order to defeat the tendency to cultivate a smaller area more intensively; and (2) to introduce some measure of compulsion, with penalties for farmers exceeding their crop quotas. The specific measures vary from crop to crop and year to year. Although reliance has in the main been placed on reduction in supply as a method of raising

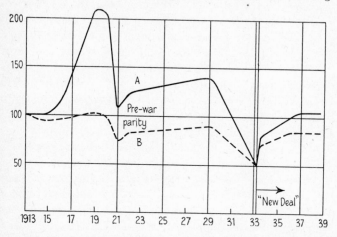

12. The changing fortunes of the American farmer. (A) shows the course of agricultural prices since 1913, (B) the relation between these prices and the prices of the industrial products the farmer buys. In 1932 a sack of corn or pound of bacon would buy only half as many implements or clothes as in 1913. One of the aims of the New Deal has been to restore the relation between farm and industrial prices to the pre-World War parity, which would mean raising the (B) curve to the level of 100.

prices, an effort has been made to increase demand as well. Foodstuffs have been purchased by the Government for distribution to persons on relief; and large stocks have been accumulated. Recently the prices of some commodities have been pegged by Federal loans on the security of crops; the price of a bale of cotton does not fall below the amount the Government is willing to lend on it.

In apparent contradiction to the crop limitation programme the Department of Agriculture has actively carried on its policy of improving methods of agriculture. Various federal agencies have been engaged in checking erosion and soil depletion, and in removing farmers from submarginal land and resettling them on better land. The Tennessee Valley Authority, which we discuss below, has co-ordinated much of this work in one of the more backward regions. The Civilian Conservation Corps, which consists of several hundred thousand unemployed youths, has been used chiefly for reforestation, terracing, and other work designed to conserve the land and the forests. The burden of farm debts has been relieved by refinancing mortgages at lower interest rates.

No one pretends that the agricultural programmes have satisfactorily solved the farm problem; they have simply made the lot of the farmer more tolerable. And this is true only of the independent farmer. Crop limitation has not helped the sharecropper or the agricultural labourer; it has, indeed, tended to make their position worse. Some economists have argued that the long-run problem can be solved only by reducing the farm population, and that the higher prices achieved by the New Deal have intensified the problem by making transfer more difficult. Certainly the higher prices of export crops, like cotton, have stimulated production abroad and largely destroyed the American farmer's remaining foreign markets (in 1932–33 the U.S. sold 45% of the cotton consumed outside America; in 1936–37, 23%). A much smaller proportion of the population than the 25% now engaged in farming could supply America's own needs of agricultural products, but a reduction in the farm population is not feasible or desirable until prosperity has been restored to the rest of the economy.

Measures to remove specific evils of the concentration of power include the vigorous enforcement of the anti-trust laws (during the last two years only), the setting up of a Securities Exchange Commission to regulate the issue of new securities and trading in old ones, and two acts specifically aimed at the private power companies—one establishing the Tennessee Valley Authority, a large scale experiment in public ownership and operation, and the other providing for the dissolution of public utility (*i.e.*, in this case, power) holding companies which serve no useful purpose.

The enforcement of the anti-trust laws, which Franklin Roosevelt inherited from Theodore Roosevelt, marks a complete break with the earlier policy of " self-government in industry " represented by N.R.A.; it has been inspired by a new body bearing the unlikely title of Temporary National Economic Committee (T.N.E.C.), and by Mr. Thurman Arnold (the author of *The Folklore of Capitalism*), who is in charge of prosecution for the Department of Justice. Its aim is to reduce certain " regulated " industrial prices in industries dominated by one or a few very large firms. The effort to raise prices which had fallen too much (like farm prices) having failed, the T.N.E.C. wants to lower the prices which have not fallen enough.

The Securities Exchange Commission has been set up with the task of ensuring that prospectuses accompanying new issues state all the relevant facts and state them correctly; and of preventing fraudulent manipulation of security prices. The Tennessee Valley Authority owns and operates a large number of hydro-electric power plants, selling the power directly to industry, farmers, and municipally owned plants which undertake urban distribution. President Roosevelt's plan was to make the costs of the Authority a " yardstick " which would enable him to demonstrate that the charges of private electric plants were excessive. The Authority is in fact charging prices well below the level of private companies, and the use of electricity has enormously increased as a result. In addition to producing power, the Authority has been made a sort of regional welfare authority, coordinating the work of other Federal and local agencies throughout the Valley. It was originally given the great Muscle Shoals dam across the Tennessee River, which had been constructed during the World War to provide power for the fixation of nitrates for munitions; and it has constructed numerous other dams on the river and its tributaries not only for electric power but also to aid in flood control and navigation. The Authority has also helped in the work of soil conservation, improvement of agricultural methods, and resettlement on better land. The industrial growth of the Valley has been very rapid since 1933. Many new aluminium and other defence plants, including the great powder plant which du Pont is building for the British at Memphis, are now being constructed there, attracted by cheap power and the six-foot Tennessee River channel.

The holding company in the private power field has frequently been a device for levying excessive charges on operating companies and for the making of profits by manipulating the values of securities. The Holding Company Act places all these companies under the control of the Securities Exchange Commission, and provides for the dissolution of those which serve no useful industrial function.

A large number of acts have attempted to reform the American banking system, but the changes which they have made have been so superficial and ineffective that they are not worth a detailed discussion. The United States has no powerful Big Five banks, but thousands of independent banks, most of them small, weak, and incapable of inspiring much confidence on the part of their depositors. The reasons for this are partly historical, partly legal. In most States banks are forbidden to establish branches outside the limits of the city in which the parent bank is located. There were thousands of failures in the 1920's; and thousands each year after the 1929 crash were a major factor in intensifying the depression and a major cause of distress. The New Deal stopped the failures by Acts which improved the banks' liquidity, and by a scheme for partially insuring deposits, which tended to discourage " runs ". It has also made certain changes in the Federal Reserve System (corresponding to the Central Banks of other countries), which facilitate its control of credit. But the American banking system remains in much the same chaotic state as the great depression found it. There are fewer banks, because so many have failed, but there are still about 15,000. These are united not in one system, but in forty-nine; for each of the forty-eight States has its own system, with its own regulations and inspectorate, and State banks are not required to become members of the Federal system. Many of the New Dealers believe that President Roosevelt missed his great opportunity in 1933 to introduce the drastic reforms of American banking which were and are still required.

The second task of the New Deal was to secure recovery. It has attempted to do so by increasing " purchasing power "; and after the failure of the N.R.A. to achieve this by monopolistic raising of prices, it has tried the following methods: (1) the opening of the banks, and the prevention of further failures by the methods referred to above; (2) the expansion of credit by the Federal Reserve System, and the lowering of interest rates; (3) special credit facilities to industry through the Reconstruction Finance

Corporation, and through other Federal agencies for the construction of homes and for agricultural purposes; (4) various methods, already discussed, to raise the incomes of labour and the farmer; (5) measures designed to increase exports, including the devaluation of the dollar, and the Hull Reciprocal Trade Treaties, which provided for reciprocal lowering of tariffs; and (6) relief and public works on a massive scale. It was hoped that the increased purchasing power resulting from these measures would increase production, and at the same time the general level of prices, which would make tolerable the burden of debt inherited from the 1920's.

The opening of the banks was accomplished, but this was a negative achievement. The Federal Reserve effectively lowered interest rates, but these failed to attract industrial or commercial borrowers. The Reconstruction Finance Corporation lent chiefly for the purpose of refinancing, and was responsible for little new construction or employment. The special measures to stimulate residential building by reducing costs and making funds available at low interest rates were not very successful. Private construction remained the most depressed of all industries. Raising wage *rates* and the prices of farm commodities is, as the New Dealers discovered, a very dubious method of increasing purchasing power in general. Export trade was expanded from the lowest levels of the depression, but the increase did not amount to much while Europe remained at peace. Such recovery as the New Deal was able to accomplish resulted very largely from its expenditure on relief and public works, financed by large-scale borrowing.

The Federal Government had never before undertaken responsibility for relief, which had been left to the States and municipalities to deal with in a very haphazard fashion. The New Deal has effectively

VIII. NEW DEAL PUBLIC WORKS

1. BOULDER DAM (*Fairchild Aerial Surveys, Inc.*)

2. W.P.A. WORKERS (*John Carsten Hatlem*)

transferred the major part of the responsibility to the Federal Government, which has exercised it in three ways: (1) by direct outdoor relief, usually through local agencies which are subsidized; (2) by temporary part time employment on what are now called W.P.A. (Works Progress Administration) projects; and (3) by public works, under the P.W.A. (Public Works Administration). The W.P.A. does minor local jobs, and attempts to employ as much labour and as little capital as possible; its critics refer contemptuously to its projects as " boondoggling ". The P.W.A. undertakes larger works—construction of dams, new highways, buildings of various kinds—and attempts to do them in the most efficient way. The most spectacular achievements of the P.W.A. have been the great dams across the Colorado River at Boulder and the Columbia River at Grand Coulée and Bonneville, the massive new Government buildings in Washington, many of which were required to house the new authorities created by the New Deal, and the largest bridges in the world across the Hudson River and San Francisco Bay. But it has also built numerous Federal Buildings and post offices, municipal power plants, schools, sewage systems, highways, tunnels, and bridges throughout the country. The Federal Government has become by far the nation's largest employer; at the peak, in 1936, it employed directly 3,000,000 in the W.P.A., 500,000 in the Civilian Conservation Corps, and 300,000 in the P.W.A., in addition to more than 1,000,000 in the civil service and the armed forces.

This enormous expenditure on public works and relief has had some effect on business activity; it has not secured the desired recovery because it has not led to increased private expenditure on construction and capital goods. Expenditure and employment may be divided into three types: that on consumption goods and services (*e.g.*, food, clothes, furniture, gadgets); that on construction and capital goods (residences, factories and machines); and public. The boom of the 1920's was supported by large scale investment in private capital (*i.e.*, expenditure of the second type), and the increase in public expenditure under Roosevelt, while on a large scale by former standards, was not sufficient in itself to take its place.

Graph 13 (curve B) shows the total expenditure of the

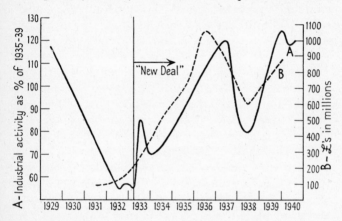

13. The Great Depression in the United States. (A) is the Federal Reserve Board's index of industrial production. (B) shows the magnitude of Federal Government expenditures on public works, relief, and the "soldiers' bonus" which were partly designed to "prime the pump" for recovery.

Federal Government on relief, public works, and the bonus for ex-soldiers: this was the expenditure which New Dealers hoped would "prime the pump"; *i.e.*, stimulate private construction and other private investment. It did not do so, although the very close correspondence between the changes in its amount and the level of business activity (curve A in Graph 13), suggest that its direct effects were the chief factor in determining this level. The total Roosevelt deficit has been of the order of £1,000 millions a year (*i.e.*, somewhat greater than the special expenditure shown on Graph 13, although it fluctuated in much the same way). Judging by the spending habits of the 1920's a deficit of at least three times this magnitude would have been necessary, without private investment on a substantial scale, to restore activity to boom levels.

There have been several attempts to explain why Government spending on this large scale failed to stimulate private capital investment. Those who subscribe to the theory of the " mature economy ", including some New Dealers, say that the frontiers of new investment have disappeared. They maintain, not very plausibly, that the boom of the 1920's had left America with a surplus of capital of all kinds. Other New Dealers have accused capital of a " sit-down strike ", with a view to discrediting the New Deal. Conservatives have retorted that private investment has been held back by justified fears of oppressive regulation and heavy taxation. Whatever the reason or reasons, private investment and construction has remained at a very low level, and unemployment has not declined much below the level of 10,000,000. There was the short lived N.R.A. boomlet in 1934 while manufacturers and traders were building up stocks in expectation of higher prices, and a more substantial one in 1937 as Federal spending reached its peak ($4,000 million was distributed in 1936–37 as a bonus to ex-soldiers), but no broad or sustained recovery.

This, then, is the *economic* record of the New Deal. It found the United States the most backward of Western countries in its social legislation. It has done much to enable America to catch up with other progressive countries; and most of the reforms which it has introduced will endure in modified form. But it has created no new economic society. The American economy of 1940 is the American economy of 1930 slightly modified. The New York Stock Exchange behaves in more seemly fashion, and the power holding companies are mildly chastened, but the 200 corporations are almost as powerful as they were in 1929, and 15 of them, according to the T.N.E.C., are still controlled by three families—the du Ponts, Mellons, and Rockefellers. Labour and the farmer have been given a little more power and a good deal more security. Social security and the assumption of responsibility for relief by the Federal Government have prevented much destitution which the greatest depression would otherwise have caused. But the depression has persisted, and its effects have been at least as considerable as those of the New Deal which failed to conquer it. It has destroyed the ambitions of enough labourers to make effective trade unionism practicable in the mass production industries. It has slowed down the replacement of machinery, a much larger proportion of which is now obsolescent than in 1929. It has retarded the acquisition of industrial skill by millions of new entrants into industry, and caused more millions to lose in their idleness much of the industrial skill which they once possessed.

More important than the effects on the economy have been the effects on attitudes: The New Deal has been called a revolution in ideas rather than in economics, although it is difficult to disentangle the joint influences of the New Deal and the depression in the change in ideas which has occurred. So large a section of American opinion is now convinced that the Federal Government ought to intervene in economic matters—to help business and the farmer, to protect investors and depositors, to insure labour's right to organize and bargain, to prevent privation, to give the idle useful work—that one of the major parties (the Democratic) is definitely committed to the policy, and the other (the Republican) scarcely dares to criticize it. This is a far cry from the " rugged individualism " of the 1920's, when the popular slogan was " More business in government, less government in business ".

Even the change in attitudes, however, must not be exaggerated. A recent survey by *Fortune Magazine*, based on a careful sampling of public opinion, shows that neither the individualism nor the optimism of the 1920's has entirely disappeared. The typical American still considers himself a member of the middle class, who would like to go into business for himself, and expects to some time, who considers the interests of employers and employees basically the same, and would prefer private to government employment. Most significantly of all, perhaps, after ten years of depression, almost three-fifths consider their opportunities to be greater than those of their fathers, and over three-fifths say that they would prefer "a job that pays a high wage, but with a fifty-fifty chance of getting promoted or fired, to a steady job earning just enough to get by on, but with no prospect for advancement ". The frontier may have disappeared in fact, but most Americans refuse to admit it.

CHAPTER VI

WAR

THE most important impact of the war on the American economy so far has been on foreign trade; and here not so much on its amount as on its direction and character.

American foreign trade in the middle of the nineteenth century was of the greatest importance in securing and maintaining a high standard of life. The export trade consisted primarily of agricultural products, of which cotton and the grains were the chief, while the major imports were finished products and capital goods. The heavy British and European demand for food and raw materials, coupled with the fact that America was the first great overseas supplier of these things to be developed, made primary exports highly remunerative. During the second half of the nineteenth century over 75% of American exports were of agricultural products (see Graph 14A). The growth of American industry and the development of new overseas sources of raw materials caused this proportion to fall steadily from about 1890, and at the beginning of the war agricultural exports were a bare quarter of the total. The remainder consisted chiefly of finished or semi-finished industrial products, of which the most important, in order, were motor-cars and parts (over 10% of the total), iron and steel, industrial machinery, and electrical machinery and apparatus. The "infant industry" argument for tariffs had apparently been fully vindicated, although much the same development would doubtless have occurred, at a somewhat slower pace, without protection.

Accompanying this change in the character of exports was a corresponding change in the character of imports: a shift from finished products to the raw materials and foodstuffs which America did not produce, or produced in inadequate quantities—sugar, coffee, tropical fruits and oilseeds, rubber, and tin. And the change in the character of the trade was

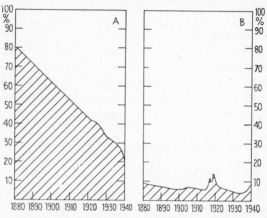

14. American foreign trade. The shaded area in (A) shows agricultural exports as a proportion of total exports. The shaded area in (B) shows total exports as a proportion of total national production. Imports were throughout the period smaller than exports.

responsible for a change in its direction. Although Europe continued to take more U.S. exports than any other single continent, its proportion in the total steadily declined. At the beginning of the war almost half of American foreign trade was with the undeveloped countries of Latin America, Africa, and Oceania, which stood in much the same relation to the United States as the United States to nineteenth century Europe.

The war has, on the whole, intensified this trend.

It has closed most European markets for American raw materials—first Germany, then German occupied territory, then Italy, and now virtually the whole of the continent except Great Britain. At the same time it has reduced the competition of European exports in undeveloped countries, which now have to rely almost exclusively on Great Britain and Japan, whose resources are pretty fully employed elsewhere, and the United States. Great Britain, it is true, is continuing to make large-scale purchases in the United States, but they are purchases of planes, machinery, and industrial products. To conserve her supplies of foreign exchange, which are large but not unlimited, she is relying to the greatest possible extent on Empire sources of raw materials and foodstuffs. The result is that while total exports have risen substantially since before the war, the gains have been confined to finished materials of war, machinery and semi-manufactured goods needed for war production, and industrial products. Exports of food have declined to almost nothing; oil exports have declined; cotton exports were maintained for a time, but they too are likely to decline; tobacco, of which one-third is normally exported, has suffered more than any other commodity. The total effects of the war on American foreign trade are revealed by the figures for the first half of 1940: exports were just over $2,000 million, 46% higher than in the corresponding months of 1939; total imports were about $1,200 million, the gain of 18% reflecting chiefly increases in prices, and in part purchases for stock of strategic materials, which were just beginning in this period.

It would be useless to pay too much attention to detailed figures, because the situation is changing so rapidly. The entry of Italy into the war and the defeat of France have already made conditions very different from those which existed during most of the first half of 1940. Nevertheless, it is difficult to foresee any developments which would interfere seriously with these trends in the near future. America may extend the ban on the export of strategic materials, already partially applied to scrap iron and aviation petrol. But there will remain many things which the belligerent countries will continue to buy; and it seems probable that Great Britain will increase her purchases to such an extent as to more than make good the removal of France from the export area. As long as the war retains anything like its present character exports of agricultural products will remain very low, and exports of industrial products, particularly machines and military products, as well as total exports, will remain high. Imports will undoubtedly increase over the figure for the first half of 1940, for the purchase of strategic materials is being intensified.

The second effect of the war on the American economy has been to increase the output and prosperity of certain industries, and to a minor extent as yet, industry in general. The industries most affected so far are those producing steel, machines, machine tools, ships and 'planes; *i.e.*, those producing for export to the belligerents. Employment in aircraft production in June 1940 was two and a half times what it was at the beginning of 1939, and in machine tools twice as great. The steel industry is operating at full capacity. American rearmament will increase activity in these industries and in many others. Orders are just being placed, and the only industry greatly affected so far is shipbuilding, where employment is almost doubling in each twelve months. But an expenditure of over $10,000 millions (£2,500 millions) has been sanctioned, and the effects will be felt not only in 'planes, machines, machine tools, iron and steel, and the naval dockyards, but also in motor-cars, chemicals, arms plants, and all the industries which supply them.

The direct effects of the increase in exports on general production and prosperity should not be exaggerated. American exports in recent years have amounted to only about 5% of total production (see Graph 14B), and an increase of 50% or even 100% in their quantity would not produce anything approaching a boom. The effects of exports on industry in general are analogous to those of Government spending on public works; and the increase in exports achieved so far is less than half the level of the Federal deficit under Roosevelt, which proved to be on an entirely inadequate scale. American rearmament will add a great deal to the other stimulants—more in 1941 than the largest New Deal deficit—but it will be accompanied by some reduction in public expenditure for other purposes. Indirect effects of increased export and rearmament expenditure may, however, be extremely important. It must be remembered that American industry is probably " ripe " for a boom. Investment in manufacturing capital has been at an extremely low level for a decade: maintenance has been on an inadequate scale, and probably no new net investment has been undertaken on balance. 70% of metal working machinery is over 10 years old, compared with less than 50% in 1929, and much the same is probably true of most other industries and of the railways. Residential construction has been even more depressed than business investment; and an increase in employment in war industries would probably reveal, by shifting population and increasing earnings, how large the potential demand for housing is. There may be something to be said for the view that whereas large-scale peace-time public works tend to frighten private investors, increases in exports and expenditure on armaments tend to encourage them. Certainly, with the huge gold stock, monetary conditions are favourable for expan-

sion. It is quite possible that war will prove the
" pump primer " for which the New Dealers have
been seeking in vain.   In December 1939 the index of
industrial production passed the 1929 peak for the
first time (this represented industrial production per
head about 10% below the 1929 level), and after a
brief lapse a new and vigorous recovery was sustained
throughout 1940.

The third major effect of the war is that it has
added greatly to America's already huge stocks of
monetary gold.   U.S. exports began markedly to
exceed imports about the beginning of 1937, partly
because of the devaluation of the dollar, partly because
other countries were more prosperous than the U.S.,
and partly because they were making abnormal purchases in anticipation of war.   Since the war this gap
has been increased, and a considerable part of the
gold flow has simply represented the adverse balance
of trade of the rest of the world.   Monetary gold
being as useless to the payer as to the payee, it is
quite naturally the way in which he prefers to make
payment.   The rest of the gold flow represented a
flight of capital from Europe to America.   It was
not attracted by interest rates, because these were
lower in America than anywhere else, but by the
apparent and relative safety of dollar assets.

In 1935 the United States possessed $9.5 thousand
millions of monetary gold (in devalued dollars)—just
under half the world total.   By the outbreak of war
this had increased to $17 thousand million, or two-
thirds of the world total, and by the middle of 1940
to over $20 thousand million.

This gold has been embarrassing, to say the least,
to the Treasury and the Federal Reserve Banks.
Monetary stocks were already more than adequate in
1935; the additions since that time have been worse
than redundant, for they have created the danger of

inflation. The policy adopted has been one of
" sterilization ", which prevents the new stock serving
as a basis for an increase of money and credit. But
it is an expensive and troublesome policy: it has
involved large-scale borrowing by the Treasury to
buy gold to be interned in deep vaults in the Ken-
tucky mountains. For a completely useless asset,
which may lose even its monetary value in the future,
a heavy and continuous interest charge must be
borne.

The future gold policy of the American Government is being debated, and some people are advocating
that further imports should be refused. The root of
the difficulty is that America has never really faced
the implications of her change from a debtor to a
creditor nation which occurred at the time of the last
war. A debtor nation can sell more abroad than she
buys; a creditor nation must buy more than she
sells, or make continuing loans, or import gold indefinitely. America has found none of these courses
very palatable: she chose the alternative of lending
abroad in the 1920's, but the defaults of the '30's
discouraged further loans, and gold has since been
accepted in payment for the excess of exports.

The consequences of a ban on gold imports would
be very serious for the British Empire, which is using
gold to pay for much of the war material purchased
in the States. The alternatives to gold as a means
of payment will be discussed in the next chapter; but
they are less attractive and limited in amount. Because the United States is anxious to sell abroad, and
because a ban on gold imports would make the
British situation difficult, it is extremely unlikely that
any change in policy will be made.

CHAPTER VII

AMERICA AND THE BRITISH EMPIRE

THE present relations between America and Great Britain are, nominally at least, governed by the American Neutrality Act of November 1939. Its most important provisions exclude American ships from belligerent waters, and forbid the granting of credits of any kind for the export of war materials.

This means that Britain has to pay cash for her purchases in the United States, and must carry the materials in her own ships, or the ships of Allied or other neutral countries. So far neither the cash nor the carry provisions of the Neutrality Act have proved very onerous; cash has been available, and, with economies, British and Allied shipping has proved adequate for its task.

With credits barred there are only three ways in which the cash necessary to make purchases can be obtained. One, obviously a desirable method from the British point of view, is by exports. It is not necessary that these should go direct to the United States. Exports to third countries which in turn export to the United States, or which can make payment in gold, are just as good. The second way is by selling gold to the United States. This is, in many respects, the best method, since it does not use British resources which might be usefully employed on other phases of the war effort, but it is limited by the amount of gold possessed by Britain at the beginning of the war, and the annual output of the Empire, assuming this all to be available. The third way is by liquidating British dollar assets—deposits in American banks, loans, securities, and property.

The total amount of gold and dollar assets held by Britain is not known, but the National City Bank of New York estimates that it was only slightly less at the beginning of this war than in 1914. It estimates that total British gold, including that earmarked for British account abroad, amounted to $2,200 millions, British bank balances in the U.S. to $580 millions, and British holdings of negotiable American securities to $1,090 millions—a total of $3,870 millions, or almost £1000 millions, enough to buy more than 50,000 planes. In the first year of the war Britain imported goods worth only £200 millions from America, though orders placed were much larger.

This is by no means the limit of British resources which might be used to make American purchases. An unknown but considerable amount of British capital is directly invested in American business and property. The Empire produces annually something like $700 millions of gold, which is enough in itself to purchase all the American planes which are likely to be available for export during the next twelve months. As a last resort Britain has investments in the Dominions and the Argentine amounting to well over $6,000 millions which could be sold in the American market. Credits would be a convenience, and they would obviate the necessity of selling securities on un-favourable terms, but they are not in any sense necessary to Great Britain's war effort this year, and securing them would have very little effect on the long-run cost of the war to Britain. Perhaps the ban on credits has made the British purchasing agents in America, expecting a long war, a little too cautious in spending limited dollar assets immediately, but the most effective bottleneck has been American production.

The loss of France as an ally and the entry of Italy

into the war have fundamentally altered the relative strengths of the Axis and Allied powers, both militarily and economically. The economic consequences can be seen clearly from a comparison of the national incomes of the belligerents, shown in Graph 15. From a twofold superiority which, properly used,

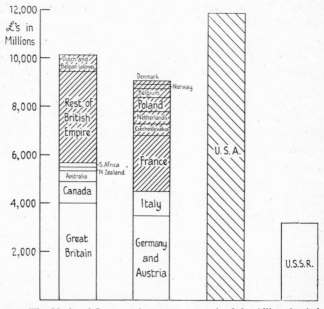

15. The National Incomes (1925–34 average) of the Allies, the Axis Powers and occupied territory, the U.S.A., and the U.S.S.R. The areas representing the colonial empires and Axis-occupied territory have been shaded because their contribution to the war effort will be less than proportional to their national incomes.

should have insured victory in the long run, the superiority of the Allies' national income has become very slight. This is true, at least, when we compare the incomes of Britain and the Dominions with those of Germany and Italy. There are additions to make on each side, and it is difficult to know how much to allow for them. On the Allied side there are the British, Netherlands, and Belgian colonial empires; on the Axis side, much of the rest of the continent, which is occupied or dominated by it. It would be a grave error to add in the national incomes of these areas without substantial qualifications. While the total income of the Allied colonial empires is high, this is very largely due to the inclusion of India and other populous Asiatic regions, and the surplus which they can contribute above their subsistence needs is small. Moreover, their industrial capacity, which is the most important factor in modern war, is almost negligible, The dominated continent, too, is likely to be worth less to the Axis than crude figures of national incomes would suggest. Apart from shortages of raw materials, which will considerably reduce the industrial contribution they could otherwise make, they will be producing under duress, and this may very adversely affect efficiency. It is impossible to draw any certain conclusions from the national income data except that neither side, in the long run, has a marked superiority of economic strength. Only by drawing on the economic resources of the rest of the world can Britain definitely tip the balance in her favour; and since the United States is the only great industrial country still non-belligerent, " the rest of the world " means, for practical purposes, the United States.

National or regional economies may be supplementary or complementary. They may produce the same sorts of things, or different sorts. An economic union of complementary economies is stronger than the sum of the strengths of the constituent economies. France and the United Kingdom had complementary economies; and it is one of the tragedies of the pre-war era that co-operation between them was not undertaken until after war was declared, and that union was not proposed until France had been beaten. The

United Kingdom and the rest of the Empire are an even better example of complementary economies: without the financial and industrial power of the United Kingdom the rest of the Empire would be an easy prey for any Great Power; without the Empire the United Kingdom would be desperately pressed for the food and raw materials necessary to sustain her industries. The various economic regions of the United States, which we discussed in Chapter I, also possess complementary economies.

But the economies of the United States and the British Empire are similar rather than complementary; their combined strengths would not be very different from the sum of their individual strengths. Each possesses great industrial and financial resources, and each is able to produce most of its essential foodstuffs and raw materials. There are exceptions, which we must consider, but in general the ability of the United States to redress the balance of power in Europe depends simply upon her total economic strength, and the speed with which she can convert it to the production of materials of war. The British Empire is a well-balanced economic unit, possessing a good deal of every essential material; all the United States can do is to increase the quantities of things the Empire needs most for the job in hand.

That the United States possesses the *potential* economic strength to redress the balance, and more, cannot be questioned. A mere glance at the American national income side by side with those of the belligerents is sufficient to demonstrate this. The fact may or may not be important. It depends upon how long the war lasts as well as upon the course of American policy. In the shorter run a comparison of this sort is grossly misleading, partly because American supplies are limited by the Empire's shortage of dollars, but chiefly because American industry is not geared to war production.

This qualification does not apply to raw materials. America can immediately supply any deficiencies in the important metals, except tin and nickel, which the Allies possess in abundance, and the ferro-alloys, which are a major American problem. America and the British Empire together control two-thirds of the world output of minerals, including a large proportion of each single important mineral. America can also supply, and is supplying, machine tools, machinery, and motor-transport vehicles. But although the major part of her production of military aircraft will probably go to Britain, the numbers will, for another year, be less than the British industry is now producing. Tanks will not be produced in quantity until 1942. Explosives will be ready more quickly, but the period of preparation will take at least a year. Rifles, guns, machine-guns, and ammunition have already been sent in fairly large quantities—exact numbers are not known, but it has been estimated in America that a fourth of the troops in Britain are now equipped with American arms, and one fears that the estimate may be right—but these deliveries have nothing to do with America's present production capacity. They were made from the very large stocks accumulated as a result of the last war. It will be at least a year before mass production makes additional supplies of any of them available in quantity.

In certain respects the economies of the United States and the British Empire are complementary; the statement that they are not is true only when broad categories of goods are considered. The United States, as we have seen, is short of tin, nickel, rubber, mercury, and most of the ferro-alloys. The British Empire has large export surpluses of the first three, as well as of some of the ferro-alloys. The British Empire, on the other hand, is short of two of the most vital materials of modern war—oil and steel. Up to the present its needs of oil have been met by supplies from Roumania, Iraq, Iran, the Netherlands East Indies, and Venezuela, in all of which many of the wells are British owned. But supplies from Roumania have been stopped, supplies from the next three depend upon the fortunes of war and diplomacy in the immediate future, and no other sources of supply outside the U.S. could fill the gap. Relatively to Germany and the countries controlled by her the British Empire is very short both of iron ore and steel-making capacity. Maximum Empire production is about 16 million tons a year, while Germany alone is capable of producing over 20 million, and the countries under her control add a further 20 million. The United States can produce at least 55 million tons, and a substantial amount, depending upon the speed of her own rearmament, can be and is being exported to Britain.

The position of the Empire *vis-à-vis* Germany and Italy is weaker in the short run than the figures of national income suggest, because the Axis Powers have spent longer preparing for the war. In the long run it is stronger than they suggest, both because a substantial part of the resources of the United States will become available, and because the Axis Powers are very short of certain important materials—a shortage which the national income figures conceal. Graph 16 shows the relative amounts of important raw materials produced by the Allies, the United States, the Axis, the rest of Europe, and Soviet Russia in 1937. The Allies are in a strong position with respect to most of the metals and rubber. The United States redresses the balance in steel. The Axis has more bauxite, but the Allies, thanks to the Netherlands Empire, have enough. The Allies, with the United States, have an abundance of oil; the Axis has little, and Russia cannot spare much for export. In addition to the commodities shown, the foodstuffs (especially the important vegetable oils) and the textiles are working on the side of the Allies; and there is no country, like the United States, capable of making good the Axis deficiencies.

The discussion so far has assumed that the United States retains her non-belligerency and her policy of " aid short of war ". If she became a belligerent the economic strength which she would add to the Allies would undoubtedly be greater—but only in the long run. She would go about the job of transferring resources to war production with greater energy.

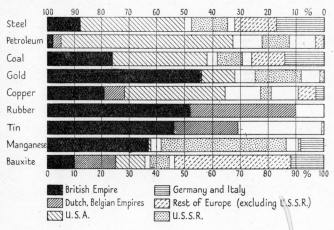

16. Control of strategic materials. The shaded areas represent the production (1937) of the British Empire, the Allied Colonial Empires, the U.S.A., the U.S.S.R., the Axis Powers, and the rest of Europe as a proportion of total world production. The unshaded areas represent the production of the rest of the world.

And there would be no difficulties, as there are at present, in securing the co-operation of industry in expanding plant and production; in war-time democratic nations accept the use of methods of coercion which they will not tolerate in time of peace.

But in the short run a declaration of war by the United States could not help the Allies very much, and might conceivably weaken them. The difficulties of securing dollars would be removed, but this is not a short-run difficulty; the bottleneck is American production rather than Allied cash. The small part of the American Navy which could be spared from the Far East and American waters could be sent to the Mediterranean, but the American Army and Air Force which would be ready for service is negligible by European standards. And there is the certainty that the equipping of an army and air force for service in the future would have the immediate effect of reducing deliveries of 'planes and other war materials to the Allies. These deliveries cannot be enormous in 1941 however energetically Americans act. The very fact that America uses mass production methods means, for reasons considered in detail in Chapter IV, that preparation for production requires a great deal of time. Any diversion of what supplies are available in this critical period might therefore prove very serious. The experience of the last war is illuminating. The quantity of American exports to Europe (allowing for changes in prices) in 1915 was 39% greater than in 1914; in 1916 it was 75% greater; in 1917, 90% greater; but in 1918, with the U.S. fully belligerent, only 27% greater. It is true that the proportion of European exports going to England and France increased from 51% to 71% over this period, but American demands on her own output nevertheless decreased the surplus available for Allied consumption. Just as the non-belligerency of Italy helped Hitler last winter more than Italy's military aid could, it is possible that non-belligerency is, from the Allied point of view, the most favourable short-run policy for the United States. This argument applies with special force to the possibility of America becoming involved in a war in the Far East. It will cease to apply, as far as the war against Hitlerism is concerned, sometime in 1942, when America's own initial force has been equipped, and her mass production industries have started to function on a war basis.

INDEX

(Graphs are indexed in italics.)

Agriculture and products, 15,
  17–22, 27–9, 32, 34–9, 45, 75–7,
  82–4, 86, 88, 95, 98
Agriculture, Department of, 35,
  84
*Agricultural productivity of selected
  countries*, 34
" Aid short of war," 109–10
Aircraft industry and production,
  14, 28, 51, 61–3, 67–70, 73, 98,
  103, 107
Allison aero engines, 69
Aluminium, 42, 57, 71, 86
American Federation of Labor, 82
American foreign trade, 96
Antimony, 42, 71–2
Anti-trust laws, 80, 85
Argentine, 35, 103
Armament industries, 14, 60–64,
  69, 98, 107
Armour-plate, 63, 66
Arnold, Thurman, *The Folklore of
  Capitalism*, 85
Assembly line method, 47, 63,
  68–9
Australia, 12, 20, 45
Average income by occupations 1935,
  21
*Average wages and incomes in G.B.
  and U.S.A.*, 22

Baker, O. E., v
Baldwin Locomotive Works, 66
Banks and banking system, 21,
  75–6, 86–8
Bauxite, 108
Bell Telephone Company, 77
Bethlehem steel plant, 63–4
Bolivia, 72
Bonneville Dam, the, 90
" Bottle-necks," 62–3, 68, 73,
  103, 110
Boulder Dam, the, 44, 90
British Malaya, 71–2
Building and construction trades,
  13 n., 18–20, 22, 39, 45, 57,
  59, 76, 78, 88, 90–91, 99
Burbank aircraft plant, 67

California, 26, 28, 37, 67
Canada, 12, 32, 40, 45, 72
Capital, accumulation of, 9, 28–
  30, 47–8
Capital and capital goods, 13 n.,
  14, 30–31, 37, 42, 46–8, 51,
  55–6, 70, 72, 78, 90–91, 95, 99
Cement, 51
Chain stores, 24
*Changing character of American in-
  dustry*, 54
*Changing fortunes of the American
  farmer*, 83
*Changing pattern of American occu-
  pations*, 18
Chemical industry, 48, 53, 57, 61,
  64, 98
Chevrolet motors, 52, 68
China, 12–13
Chromium, 42, 71–2
Churchill, Winston (the Prime
  Minister), 60–61
Citrus fruits, 21, 28, 37–8
Civilian Conservation Corps, 84,
  90
Clark, Colin, *The Conditions of
  Economic Progress*, v, 10 n.
Coal and coal industry, 14, 20, 27,
  40, 42–4, 72, 75
Columbia River dams, 44, 90
Congress of Industrial Organiza-
  tions, 82
Construction. *See* Building
Consumption and consumption
  goods, 19, 38, 48, 78, 90–91
*Consumption of energy from coal
  etc., 1937–39*, 50
Control of strategic materials, 109
Copper, 40, 42–3
Corporations, 63, 77, 93
Cotton, 27–8, 32, 36, 38–9, 71,
  83–4, 95, 97
Credits, 87, 102–3
Crop-limitation, 82–4

Dairy products, 21, 27, 37, 39
Defence expenditure in U.S., 98–9
Denmark, 35

Depression, the Great, 16, 18, 31, 39, 42, 48, 55–6, 69, 74–6, 78–9, 93–4

Destroyers, transfer of, 66

Dollar, devaluation of the, 88, 100

Douglas, Prof. Paul, v

Du Pont plant, 64, 86

Dust Bowl, the, 36

Economic power, concentration of, 76–9, 84–5, 93

" Educational orders," 63–4

Electricity and power, 13 n., 14, 35, 43–4, 48, 50, 53, 57, 77–8, 85–6, 95

Energy, 47–8, 55–6

Erosion, 35–7, 84

Exports, 15, 27–8, 32, 38–40, 43, 53, 70, 84, 88, 95–103, 108, 110

Farmers and farming, 18, 32, 34–7, 47, 75, 77–9, 82–5, 88, 93

Federal Constitution, the, 31

Federal Government, the, 31, 39, 79, 88–91, 93

Federal Maritime Commission, the, 66

Federal Reserve Banks, 100

Federal Reserve System, 87–8

Ferro-alloys, 42, 71–3, 107

Fishing industry, 17, 22

Ford, Henry, 29

Ford Motor Company, 69

Forestry and lumber, 17, 22, 26, 28, 39–40, 57

Fortune Magazine, v, 93–4

France, 12, 56, 60, 62, 64, 97–8, 103, 105

Fruits, 28, 37–8, 96

Furniture, 47, 91

Garand rifle, 64

Gas, natural, 43, 72

General Motors, 52, 62, 64, 68–9

Germany, 12, 43, 48, 60, 62–3, 67, 97, 104, 108

Glenn Martin aircraft, 68

Gold, 28, 42

Gold stocks and sterilization, 99–103

Grains, 27, 32, 34, 37, 39, 72, 93

Grand Coulée Dam, the, 90

Great Britain, 12–13, 20, 22, 24, 42–3, 45–6, 48, 57, 61–3, 67, 70–71, 74, 79, 97, 107

Great Britain, credits in U.S., 103

—— purchases from U.S., 70, 95, 97–8, 102–3

Great Depression in the U.S., 91

Great Lakes, the, 56

Great Plains, the, 27, 36

Green, William, 82

Harvard University, 55

Hercules plant, the, 64

Hindenburg, 73

Holding Companies, 52–3, 77, 85–6

Holding Companies Act, the, 86

Holland, 35

Hoover, Herbert, 54

Hull, Cordell, Reciprocal Trade Treaties, 88

Imports, 16, 26–7, 38, 40, 53, 71, 93, 95, 100–101, 103

Income, distribution of, 20, 22, 24, 26–7, 37–8, 75, 77

—— per head, 13, 16, 22, 27–8

—— per occupied person, 10–12, 14, 16–17, 22, 24, 26

—— *per occupied person in U.S.A. (1850–1937,)* 15

India, 12, 105

Industrial research, 30, 52–3

Industry, productivity of, 16, 19, 22, 24, 29–30, 37, 45–6, 50–51, 53, 55

Investment, decline in, 48, 76, 78, 92, 99

Iron, 14, 40, 42–3, 48, 56, 77, 95, 108

Italy, 97, 103–4, 108, 110

Jerome, Dr. H., v

Knudsen, William, 62

Labour, 16, 47, 57, 60–61, 63, 68–70, 76, 78–80, 82, 88, 90, 93

Lewis, John, 82

Livestock and meat, 27, 37–9, 47, 51

Lumber. *See* Forestry

Machinery, 13 n., 27, 30, 34, 46–51, 57, 68–9, 78, 91, 93, 95, 97–9, 107

Machine-tools, 51, 61, 64, 68–70, 98, 107

Maize, 37–9

Manganese, 42, 71–2
Manufacturing, Census of, 1879, 48
Manufacturing industries and goods, 9–10, 13, 16–20, 22, 24, 27, 29, 31–2, 37, 42, 45–8, 50, 55–7, 60, 97
Mass production, 31, 50–51, 63, 67, 70, 93, 107, 110
Mercury, 42, 71, 107
Middle States, 21, 27, 31–2, 37, 75
Midvale steel plant, 63–4
Milk, 37–8
Mills, F. C., v
Mining and minerals, 18–20, 22, 27–9, 32, 40, 42–3, 45–6, 57, 107
Motor-car industry, 14, 17, 19, 47, 51–2, 57, 61–3, 67–8, 70, 77–8, 95, 98
Motor torpedo boats, 63
Munitions, 60–64, 86, 107
Muscle Shoals dam, 86

National City Bank, N.Y., 103
National Defense Advisory Commission, 62, 67, 69–70, 72–3
National incomes, 10–13, 27, 60, 104–6, 108
National Incomes (1925–34 average), 11
National Incomes (1925–34 average) of the Allies, Axis, etc., 104
National Recovery Act (1933), the, 80, 82
National Recovery Administration, 80, 85, 87, 92
Netherlands East Indies, 71–2, 105, 108
Neutrality Act (1939), the, 102
New Deal, the, 74, 76–80, 82, 84, 87–8, 90–3, 99–100
New England, 26, 29
New Zealand, 12, 20, 45
Nickel, 42, 71–2, 107
Non-belligerency policy, 109–10
Non-ferrous metals, 48, 57
North-east region, 26–7, 31

Occupations, 17–22, 24, 27–8, 42, 74–5
Oil and petroleum, 14, 27–8, 40, 42–4, 51, 53, 71–2, 77, 97–8, 107–8
Orr, Sir John, " optimum diet," 38

Pacific North-west, 26, 28
Paper, 40, 51, 57
Petroleum. *See* Oil
Physical volume of production and productivity, etc., 55
Pratt and Whitney aero engines, 68
Precision instruments, 64, 69
Prices, 10, 20, 45, 47, 77–8, 80, 85, 87–8, 92, 110
Production and war effort, 14, 59–61, 97, 106, 109
——, economies of large-scale, 50–52, 56–7
Productivity per head, 16, 45–6
Public works, 48, 88, 90–91, 99
Public Works Administration, 90
Public utilities, 48, 52–3, 85
" Pump-priming," 91, 100

Radio City, 59
R.A.F., 60–61
Railways, 13 n., 30–31, 48, 56, 78, 99
Raw materials, 26, 38, 45, 60–61, 69–71, 95–7, 105–8
Rayon, 71
Rearmament in U.S., 98–9, 108, 110
Reconstruction Finance Corporation, 71, 87–8
Regional variations in income, 1937, 26
Regions, economic, 20–21, 24, 26–8, 31, 35–6, 74, 105–6
Relief, public, 79–80, 83, 88, 90–91, 93
Rocky Mountains, 27
Rolls Royce aero engines, 69
Roosevelt, President F. D., 67, 74–6, 79, 85, 87, 91, 99
Roumania, 108
Rubber, 38–9, 53, 56, 71–2, 96, 107–8

Securities Exchange Commission, 85–6
Service industries, 9–10, 12–13, 16–17, 19, 22, 24, 28–9, 32, 42, 60, 91
Sharecroppers, 36, 84
Ships and shipbuilding, 20, 56, 61, 66–7, 98, 102
Silk, 38–9, 53, 71
Silver, 42
Social Security, 92–3

Social Security Act, 79–80
South America, 29, 32, 40
South-east region (" South "), 21, 26–7, 31–2, 35–6, 75
South-west region, 26–7
Standards of living, 9, 14, 17, 26, 29–30, 32, 95
Steel and steel industry, 14, 19, 27, 42, 46, 48, 51, 54, 56–7, 61–4, 66, 71, 73, 77, 95, 98, 108
Steinbeck, J., *The Grapes of Wrath*, 36
Stettinius, Edward, 62
Stock exchange, the, 75, 77, 93
Sugar, 38, 96
Supreme Court, the, 81

Tanks, 14, 61, 63–4, 107
Tariffs, 31, 88
Taylor, Frederick, 53–4
Temporary National Economic Committee, 85, 93
Tennessee Valley Authority, 44, 69, 84–6
Texas, 27
Textiles and industries, 20, 27, 48, 51, 57, 75, 77, 109
Time and Life Building, 59
Tin, 42, 46, 71–2, 96, 107
Tobacco, 27, 36, 38, 57, 97
Toluol (for T.N.T.), 71
Trade unions, 30, 79, 81–2, 93
Transport, 19, 31
Tungsten, 42, 71–2

Unemployment, 10–13, 15–16, 18–19, 24, 36, 38, 75–6, 79–80
U.S.A. proportion of world output, etc., 40
U.S. Air Force, 61–2, 110
—— Army, 61–4, 110
—— Navy, 61–2, 66, 110
U.S. Shipbuilding Corporation, 66
U.S. Steel Corporation, 62
U.S.S.R., the, 12, 40, 108

" Value added by manufacture," 45–6, 55, 57
Vegetables, 28, 37, 72
Vickers, 62

Wages, 22, 24, 29, 37, 46, 79, 81, 88
Wages and Hours Act (1938), the, 81
Wagner Act (1935), the, 81
War (1914–1918), 14, 20, 36, 42–3, 51, 55, 61–2, 64, 66–7, 73, 82, 86, 103, 107, 110
—— (1939–), 62, 66–7, 69–70, 72, 95–101, 103, 108–10
War Industries Board, 1918, 73
Water power, 43–4, 86
Wheat, 28, 37–9
Wisconsin, 80
Wood-pulp, 39–40, 51
Wool, 38, 71
Works Progress Administration, 90
Wright aero engines, 68

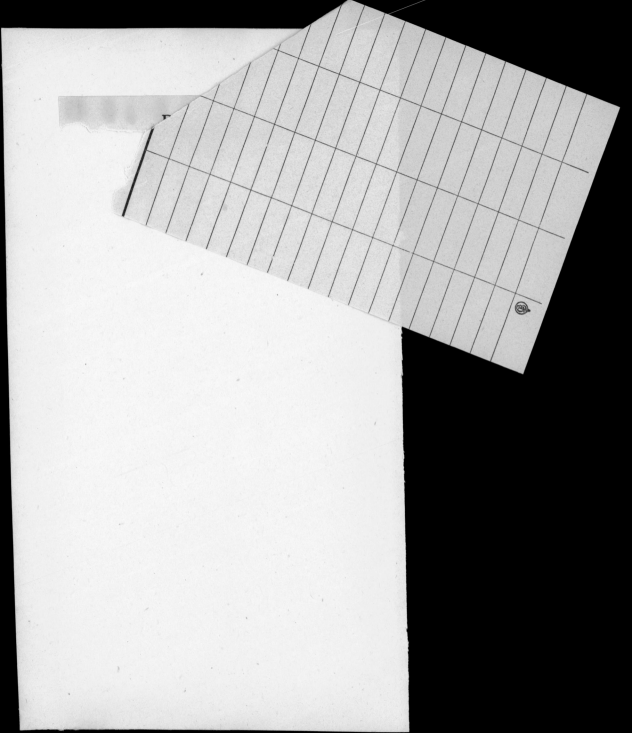